RETURN TO THE SHTETL

A Journal of My Trip to
Russia and Belarus

by
Dorothy Sucher

Edited, with an introduction
by Joseph Sucher

Summit Crossroads Press
First-Person History Series
Columbia, Maryland, USA

Published in the United States of America by
    Summit Crossroads Press
    Columbia, Maryland
    E-mail Address: sumcross@aol.com

The editor can be reached at jsucher@umd.edu.

ISBN: 978-0-9614519-1-2
Library of Congress Control No. 2015954937

IN MEMORIAM

My daughter Anne Ellen Sucher, 1966-2006, poet,
My son Michael Edward Sucher, 1958-2008, musician,
and
My wife Dorothy Glassman Sucher, 1933-2010, writer.

Table of Contents

Preface

The purpose of this book is to make available to a wide audience the journal kept by my late wife, the writer Dorothy Sucher, during a trip she took to Belarus, in the summer of 1992, in search of her family's roots. In subsequent years she read portions of it to a variety of audiences, who were spellbound and strongly moved by both the subject matter and her presentation. But she never found the time to prepare it for publication.

In the Introduction on the facing page, I give a sketch of Dorothy's life and works. This is followed by the Prologue, which is taken from one of her public presentations in which she explains how she came to make this trip. This is followed by the journal itself.

Joseph Sucher, October 2015
Silver Spring, Maryland

Acknowledgment

I would like to express my gratitude to my son Anatol Sucher, without whom this work could not have been completed. I thank Sophie Cook, Anita Landa, and Walter Rybeck for advice and many friends for their encouragement.

Introduction: Dorothy Sucher

Dorothy Glassman Sucher was born in Brooklyn, New York on May 18, 1933. She was the only child of Shirley Hankin and Henry Glassman. Her parents divorced in 1936 and she was brought up by her mother in an extended Jewish family. She was a very precocious child, with a stratospheric IQ and evident talents in writing and painting; although the application deadline had passed, her mother, a woman of great determination, managed nevertheless to get her admitted to the High School of Music and Art, then located in upper Manhattan. This required a 3-hour round trip, but Dorothy was unfazed by this and indeed flourished there, majoring in art and becoming Editor of the Yearbook.

We met at Brooklyn College in December 1951, were engaged within two weeks, and married in August 1952. While I was working towards a Ph.D. degree in physics at Columbia University, she pursued a Master's degree in English. In 1956 we had our first child and in 1957 we moved to Greenbelt, MD, to be close to the University of Maryland at College Park, where I had obtained a faculty position in the Physics Department.

Dorothy joined the *Greenbelt News Review*, a non-profit newspaper that recorded the events in this exceptional town, which began life during the 1930's as a New-Deal housing project and was denounced as socialism by right-wing politicians. Dorothy was a reporter, feature writer, and sometimes editor of this weekly for most of the 40 years we lived in Greenbelt and it was there that she honed her writing skills.

During her association with the *News Review*, Dorothy became involved with a celebrated case known as *The Greenbelt News Review v. Bresler*. She had reported the speech of citizens during a meeting of the Town Council which involved a discussion of a proposal by Charles Bresler, a local developer who was willing to sell the city a piece of land for building a school only if the city would in turn cede to him certain land which he wanted for development. Dorothy's article cited some citizens who had said that Bresler was blackmailing the city and Bresler responded by suing the Editor and the paper for 2 million dollars each for libel, claiming that he had been accused of the crime of blackmail. The paper lost both in the local county court and in the Maryland Appeals court. After a four-year battle supported by the *Washington Post*, who supplied one of their lawyers pro bono, the previous decisions were overturned by a 9-0 vote of the United States Supreme Court, holding that citing her article was protected by the First Amendment.

This case is considered as second in importance only to *New York Times Co. v. Sullivan* in the context of the First Amendment and the Freedom of the Press and is taught in law schools. When Dorothy died, full-length obituaries were written about her in the *New York Times*, the *Washington Post*, and a number of other newspapers. On September 5, 2010, she was featured briefly in the "In Memoriam" section of the weekly TV program of Christiane Amanpour, which noted the passing of people who had made significant contributions to freedom of the press.

As our family grew, we needed a larger house and Dorothy read dozens of books on building a house and drew plans for presentation to an architect. When our contractor saw them he said: "These are so good, you don't need an architect!"

When our children were old enough, Dorothy, who had always been interested in buildings, went to architecture school at the then newly opened venue at the University of Maryland, the only woman in her class, twice the age of her classmates. She was soon recognized as one of the outstanding students; her solution for building a playhouse in a neglected suburban area became the basis for an actual construction. But after two years she decided that this field, in which at the time there were very few women, was not for her, and she became interested in psychology.

After a stint of volunteering on the University of Maryland hotline, she enrolled in a small but select new program at John's Hopkins University designed to train adults to become psychotherapists, with credit given for "life experience." She obtained an MMH (Master of Mental Health) degree and practiced psychotherapy at the Washington-based GHA (Group Health Association) for a number of years. Later she saw clients privately at our Greenbelt residence and used her expertise in group therapy to make early major contributions to the Women's Movement, leading an intensive "Consciousness Raising Group," becoming the Northern Prince Georges County representative of the Maryland chapter of NOW (National Organization for Women), and one of the local organizers of the 1978 march for the ERA (Equal Rights Amendment) in Washington.

However, at some point Dorothy realized that what she had always wanted to do, since her teenage years, was to write a book, and if not now when? She loved mystery stories and decided to write one, called *Dead Men Don't Give Seminars*, based in part on our experiences at a Physics Summer Institute in Aspen. This book, involving the murder of a Nobel Prize winning physicist, was praised by one reviewer as showing "penetrating psychological insight," and she became in 1986 one of only five finalists for the Agatha Prize, which focuses on the genre made famous by Agatha Christie. She wrote another mystery, *Dead Men Don't Marry,* and founded the local chapter of SINC (Sisters in Crime), an organization of women mystery writers which has done much to level the playing field with regard to the attention paid to the work of women by publishers, reviewers, and the general public.

Her next book, her magnum opus, was called *The Invisible Garden*. This was a collection of essays about gardeners and their gardens, based on the many gardeners she had met and befriended in Cabot, Vermont, where we had a house for many years and where Dorothy, a city kid, was able to create a many-faceted garden, including a pond, which to many seemed a minor paradise. This book received rave reviews and confirmed her decision to become a full-time writer.

For some years Dorothy had been thinking about writing a book based on the experiences of her maternal grandparents, who had emigrated from Belarus in the early nineteen hundreds. When, in 1992, an opportunity to visit Belarus arose—described by her in the Prologue which follows this Introduction—she grabbed it. Except for minor corrections, the words on the succeeding pages all belong to her. Most of the pictures in the Journal which follows the Prologue were taken by Dorothy and included in the talks she gave about her journey.

Dorothy Sucher died in 2010 at age 77, of a virulent form of thyroid cancer. The seeds of this may have been sown during her post-Chernobyl visit to Belarus. Sometime later, a friend of ours said to me: "Your wife was a spectacular woman." And so she was.

—*Joseph Sucher, Editor*

Prologue

I made this journey in 1992, when I was 59 years old. Actually, though, the roots of it go back to my Brooklyn childhood, half a century earlier. I grew up in an extended family and the central figure was my grandfather Max, or Meyer as my grandmother called him. He had emigrated from Russia around 1905, and sent for his wife and son, and then other family members as soon as he could afford it. Growing up I was surrounded by a community of immigrant Jews who called themselves the Streshiners, and used to gather at my grandfather's house four times a year.

My mother sits on the lap of her father, Max Hankin.

Although I lost contact with these people many years ago, in my fifty-ninth year, old vivid memories of them suddenly began to intrude into my otherwise peaceful life. These flashbacks would appear at odd moments, when I was drifting off to sleep or stuck in traffic on the Beltway. Without warning, my mind would slip back into the distant past and it was as if I could see it all again.

People are streaming into my grandparents' house, pounding down the steps, and crowding into the special kitchen in the cellar that was used for big gatherings. The men went straight through into the "finished basement," where my grandfather had built benches against the walls, and started setting up the long tables, planks laid on saw-horses and covered with overlapping tablecloths.

The women started cooking right away, as soon as they'd set down their bundles. To me these women seemed giants, with their massive busts and heavy arms. They emptied their bags of silverware and tablecloths and platters of food. They slipped capacious aprons over their heads to save their good dresses. Steam rose from cauldrons of bubbling fish stock where gefilte fish and carrot slices danced with the heads of carp to strengthen the broth. As the back door opened and closed, blasts of cold air knifed through the rich, animal smell of pot roast and the sweet-and-sour aroma of cabbage borscht. Flushed faces hung in the steam, big spoons stirred the pots, and men wandered in from the other room to grab a taste, the women slapping their hands away playfully. There was a Babel of Yiddish and English, of loud voices, rising inflections, and foreign accents. Hands waved wildly and passions rose as the orgy of cooking mounted to a frenzy—it was late! The meeting would start!—and in the crowded kitchen elbows jostled and food was spilled, accusations of stupidity were tossed about—shlemihl! shlemazl!—and tirades and curses flew—a cholera on you! You should go in the earth!

There was such abundance, so many platters of coleslaw and bowls of dill pickles, so many knaidlach, so many rolls of stuffed cabbage, such excess of everything, the excess of those who have known what it is to subsist on apples and potatoes, whose children have gone without bread.

From my earliest years I'd been aware of "the Streshiners." All I knew about them was that they'd come from a village called Streshin, somewhere in Russia. They were forever grabbing me and pulling me close to them as if I belonged to them. They patted my bottom, fingered the texture of my hair like yard goods in a shop, and pinched my cheeks painfully. The Streshiners would stare at me with a ravenous intensity that had something satisfied and, ultimately, benevolent in it, as if they saw in me the proof of their own survival and the promise of prosperity to come—theirs, mine, it was all the same.

Yet always in the background I sensed a vague threat hanging over them—and over me. Somewhere, something terrible was happening that confused and frightened me, and as I grew older I protected myself by turning my back on the Streshiners. They were so foreign, so old-fashioned, so melodramatic, so Jewish, so boring, so totally not me. They were irrelevant to my life as a smart girl in America, and once I left Brooklyn I hardly gave them a thought.

Only now in my fifty-ninth year they'd come back to haunt me.

I hauled out a box of old photos and pored over them. The earliest went back a century and had been taken in Russia. In the evenings after work I read old letters and books of Jewish history. I studied maps and located Streshin, a tiny dot at the confluence of two blue threads, the Dnieper and Berezina Rivers. Streshin was in what used to be called White Russia and now was known as Belarus. I visited relatives I hadn't seen in years and asked if they could identify people in the old photographs. A stern-looking woman swathed completely in black turned out to be my great-grandmother, Esther Basia.

I played with the photographs for hours, as I'd done when I was a child. But back then they had remained two-dimensional and static, lying on the surfaces of the paper like dead things. Now, however, it was as if something in the pictures had lain dormant all these years, like those seeds or spores that can still grow after decades in the desert. To justify my obsession, I told myself that one day I would write a historical novel about my grandfather's life. But I doubted I was equal to the task. I knew little about Jewish history. I couldn't read or speak Yiddish. This was not my material.

***

That summer my husband and I went to Stockholm, where Joe would be giving lectures in physics. When I looked at the map I realized I was closer to Belarus than I'd ever been before. Maybe I should really try to visit Streshin. But 1992 was a bad time for travel to Russia. The Soviet Union had just broken up, the economy had collapsed, crime was rampant, and people were desperate. I was afraid to go, and my qualms went deeper than the current situation, all the way to my memories of the Streshiners. Yes, they'd spoken of the Old Country with nostalgia, but none of them had ever gone back. Russia was the prison from which they'd managed to escape, the land where the Jews had been hunted, humiliated, and murdered in pogroms.

I didn't want to know how it felt to be a Jew in Russia, where open anti-Semitism was still rampant. I didn't want to experience that much vulnerability, although in a sense I was already acquainted with it. I was an assimilated American, yet I'd had a few brushes with anti-Semitism. Past ages had laid down their deposit in my bones: the sense that to be a Jew is to be "other," and that everything one has is temporary and can be taken away in an instant. A deep vein of insecurity was a part of my Jewish heritage.

No, I didn't want to go to Streshin. In addition to everything else, the town was only about 40 miles downwind from Chernobyl, and the area had received a heavy dose of radioactivity. This summer forest fires were raging in Belarus due to a drought, releasing radioactivity into the air.

Yet once I had arrived in Sweden I couldn't help toying with the idea of going to Russia. I soon learned that there were many obstacles to doing so on short notice, but one by one they fell away. It was as if I were being swept along by a wave too strong to resist. I'd never had such an experience before.

I'm not inclined toward mysticism. Still, at this one time in my life I had a strong feeling that something was "meant to be." Maybe the God I'd ignored all those years had some inscrutable plan for me. Maybe my visit would have an effect on the life of someone I was going to meet, start some chain of events in motion. A pebble dropped in a pond doesn't know where the ripples will wash up.

My husband didn't want me to go, but once it became clear that I was going he contacted a physicist friend of ours in Russia who managed to find me a guide, a 35-year-old physicist who lived in Minsk, spoke English, and had a car.

The Streshiners

I. Stockholm Before the Trip

August 5, 1992. Without making a decision—will I go or won't I?—I seem to be edging closer to a journey to Russia. Bought a map of western Russia in the Copenhagen railway station the other day. Streshin is on it, in very small letters. Judy Narrowe, the wife of the rabbi of Stockholm, gave me the name of a travel agency. She recently returned from a trip to Gomel to bring a group of Jewish "Children of Chernobyl" to a summer camp in Sweden. I'd never heard of Gomel, but I see it's not far from Streshin; she says it's the second biggest city in Belarus, after Minsk. The agency she recommended specializes in trips to Israel, though not exclusively, and the staff are Jewish.

I like the idea of dealing with Jews; I won't have to make a lot of explanations. A helpful agent named Maria told me I could fly via Aeroflot from Stockholm to Gomel for about $500 (American); I would change in Moscow. The two legs of the journey are four hours and an hour, respectively. Close! I may try and make a reservation tomorrow. She says it's not hard to book flights to Russia, but flights out are another story! This is the kind of remark that makes me feel I shouldn't go.

I called the Russian embassy, and Intourist. I'll need a visa (10 days' notice), and according to them, to get it I must have either an "official invitation" or a prepaid hotel reservation with Intourist for every night. The trouble is, Intourist has no hotel in Gomel or Bobruisk, either of which is only about 30 miles from Streshin and would be a reasonable base of operations; they offered me the Hotel Yeleneskaya (?) in Minsk, which is over a hundred miles away. This is clearly impossible.

Strange how the name "Gomel," totally unknown to me a few days ago, has come to loom large in my life.

Maria called me back today and told me there is a travel agency that can get the visa for me, at a charge of 200 kroner ($30). Why didn't the embassy mention that possibility? Oh well, might as well do it tomorrow—it isn't much money and it commits me to nothing.

The melancholy Russian tune I heard the young Russians playing on the street in

Copenhagen keeps running through my head. I wish I knew its name. God, how those balalaikas gave me the shivers—I literally couldn't move. Kept thinking my grandfather must have heard this music as a boy, and his father and grandfather before him. But what did it mean to them? Enemy music? It was so beautiful and so sad.

The chief problem would be to find a trustworthy Russian, preferably Jewish, to be my companion and guide while I'm there. Without a translator, the trip wouldn't be worth making, since I neither speak nor read Russian. We do have a few Russian physicist friends, and Joe has sent out some E-mail to try and reach them.

There is also the whole question of food, especially since I would be in the Chernobyl fallout area; I've even been advised to bring water (gets heavy!). Surely that's excessive. It's also impossible. I'd throw my back out, trying to carry water for a week.

August 6, 1992. I'm amazed how many items I've already ticked off my list. Why is everything going so quickly and smoothly? Visited travel agency today and applied for visa. Bought Russian-English dictionary and "Teach Yourself Russian" book (who am I kidding?).

Before the trip: Dorothy in Stockholm

Also a 1991 guidebook. Fortunately, none of this commits me to anything. I'm acting as if I'm going, but deep down I know I'm not. It's too scary, especially alone. My friend Miriam was knocked down and had her bag stolen when she was there last year. She told me, "Don't go, this is a bad time." I keep expecting—hoping?—to come up against some big roadblock so I can throw up my hands and say, "I wanted to go to Russia, but it turned out not to be possible."

The title of the guidebook, *USSR: a Travel Survival Kit,* isn't reassuring. After reading a bit of it I am plunged in gloom. Asking myself if I'm out of my mind. The brief section on Belarus describes it as a "flat, dull republic." Minsk, apparently, has been completely rebuilt since 1944; nothing is left of the past, all was destroyed in the war. Half the city's population died, "a proportion close to its prewar Jewish population." Gomel isn't mentioned, let alone Bobruisk, Zlobin, or Streshin. Sixty miles north of Minsk, on the site of the hamlet of Khatyn, is a memorial called The Graveyard of Villages, commemorating "185 other Belarusian villages annihilated by the Germans. 'Trees of Life' (concrete posts) for a further 433 villages that were destroyed but rebuilt..."

Maybe Streshin was one of those towns, and nothing is left of it.

Why do I have to go to this flat, dull place where my ancestors were so unwelcome? To see a concrete post? To find out that "the past is a bucket of ashes"? I've already been told. Only, for me it isn't.

It will be difficult. It may be dangerous. I don't think I'm being melodramatic. Right now this is a land of chaos and desperate poverty, and I'll be carrying money and food. I've always depended on my skill with words to get around in the world and slide out of tight spots, but this is a place where I won't know the language. I don't have any other weapon. I'm even too fat to run.

These thoughts make me feel extremely vulnerable.

I don't know what I want from a trip to Streshin. I have only the vaguest ideas about what to see and do. When people ask me, my answers sound stupid. How can I tell what will interest me when I get there? Belarus may be boring; or terrifying. I'll need to have someone with me all the time. I'm afraid to be alone there.

I'm now planning (if that firm, solid word applies) to spend two days in Moscow, because yesterday Joe received a Bitnet[1] message from Boris and Nina Ioffe offering to put me up and show me around, if I come before they go on vacation. That's great. When I met them in Maryland last spring and took Nina for a swim at the Greenbelt pool, I assumed I'd never see them again. Amazing how things come around.

Of course this means if I go, I have to leave in less than two weeks.

A friend has put me in touch with a Russian physicist in Italy. He, it turns out, has a young colleague with him who has worked in—guess where? Gomel! When I heard this I thought, Maybe this trip was meant to be.

I spoke to the student on the telephone. He swears his wife in Minsk is just the person I want—she will take care of everything! She has a car, she drives, but she doesn't speak English. No matter! She has friends who speak English! Not to worry! She will take care! Unfortunately, it is virtually impossible for him to reach Minsk by telephone from Italy. He will try though, and send me a message by e-mail.

Maybe something will come of this. The travel agent had told me how hard it is to reach Minsk or even Moscow by phone: "We have to try maybe thirty times." The Bitnet and fax are a godsend.

August 7, 1992. My feelings swing up and down wildly about this trip with every new piece of information. Joe "forgot" to tell me he'd received a reply to his Bitnet message to Lev Okun saying, "I've asked several people to establish contact with their friends in Belarus. Hope to send you positive information in a week. Best regards to Dorothy."

This cheered me up. I adored Lev when I met him in Maryland, and we decided to be cousins because his mother came from Zlobin, only ten miles from Streshin. He is very sensitive and smart, and quite famous, apparently. I wish he could show me around himself, but he's in Moscow and must be too busy.

Also there were two bitnets from the Gomel physicist:

"I have phoned to my wife. She cannot promise at once she can help you in Gomel, but she is going to consult to her friends what can be done, so don't worry. I'll phone her later again."

---

1   *An early version of e-mail communication*

And later, "Of course, if Lev Okun is going to help you, he can do it much better even from Moscow. But still I believe the help of my wife may be useful. She told me that she will meet Dorothy (I am not sure her name really Dorothy) in airport of Minsk herself (if she come to Minsk)."

This is getting serious. My travel agent is trying to get me a flight from Moscow to Minsk.

This morning there was an item in the Swedish paper datelined Gomel. Due to a drought, forest fires are raging in Belarus, releasing radioactivity from Chernobyl into the air. There are reports of people dying of heart attacks. My Swedish friend Mai-Britt, who is a doctor, says of course this has nothing to do with radiation directly but, "maybe people there are hysterical, because of the fear and the stress."

Was it Carl Sandburg who wrote, "The past is a bucket of ashes"?
Joe remarked, "When you stir the ashes and there are still sparks, you dump more ashes on top to cover them up." That's his method.
I said, "Or you can use the sparks to start a new fire in the present." That's mine.
In Belarus the ashes of the past have flared up, and the fires are radioactive.

LATER, AT THE UNIVERSITY. There was a message from Lev by E-mail.
"A person in Minsk whose name is Yaakov Mikhailovich Shnir is ready to serve as a guide. Please contact him. The next week I will be out of town. Nevertheless inform me about the matter." He gives the telephone and e-mail numbers.

Is this good news? Who is this Shnir person? Is he trustworthy? Joe says we can "absolutely" assume he is. The name is Jewish, and of course I prefer, in fact need, a Jewish guide.
It's starting to sink in that this thing has gotten out of hand. People are taking me seriously—they think I really want to go to Russia. They're doing things! Even Lev has bestirred himself, and actually come up with a name. How can I say I didn't really mean it? I can't waste the time of someone important—not to mention all the other people who've

been roped in by now. My name is going to be mud, and so is Joe's, if I keep this up.

If my mother were alive, she would tell me not to go. I'm absolutely sure of it.

Perhaps I won't get the visa in time.

Joe has sent a bitnet to Shnir giving the probable dates I'll be in Belarus and asking him to reply. No details as yet; first we want to see if he gets the message.

I have spent an hour puzzling over the Cyrillic alphabet, and still can't remember how to write my name in Russian.

Monday, August 10, 1992. Stockholm. Somewhere along the line the question ceased to be "Will I?" and became "How?" I'm accepting the fact that it's too late to back out. Too many people are already involved. After all those years in the Women's Movement I can't bring myself to give an adorable little simper and say it's a woman's prerogative to change her mind.

Though I guess I could....

I have a confirmed flight reservation to and from Moscow. Only the Belarusian part is still unconfirmed, but at worst I can just explore Moscow and maybe Leningrad. Of course, it's possible I won't get my visa. This is my only hope.

Or I could get sick.

Joe and I spent the weekend celebrating our 40th anniversary with a second honeymoon at the splendid Grand Hotel in Saltsjobaden. An exquisite room with a double bed (something we don't have in Stockholm), a view over the water with little boats bobbing up and down, my first bubble bath ever, (a packet of bubble stuff was provided by the hotel), and a leisurely dinner with a bottle of Veuve Cliquot. It was a weekend for lovers and there were lots of them wandering about, some young and others, like ourselves, rather elderly. Somehow I don't think Russia's going to be like that. The more I find out about Gomel, the more it seems to be the smelly armpit of the world.

I woke up at 3 a.m. last night and couldn't get back to sleep, so I worked on my flashcards of the Cyrillic alphabet. I'm starting to remember a few of the letters. God, it's hard—my memory has gone soft with age.

I have shopped for food to take on the trip. Since I don't know if I'll be staying in hotels, or in flats where I can cook, I'm taking enough to live on for a week, the sort of thing you might take up Mt. Everest: muesli, peanut butter, crackers, powdered milk, and various canned and dried foods. I don't want to spend all my time in Russia standing in grocery queues. My suitcase is going to weigh a ton, so I'd better take a luggage cart so I don't throw my back out again.

I've been running around to banks, changing my American money into small bills, as many singles, fives, and tens as they'll give me, plus some twenties. A thousand dollars in small bills makes a massive wad. I bought a money belt to go under my clothing, and one of those waist pouches to use instead of a pocketbook, inspired by thoughts of my friend who had her purse snatched. Let them try and get that off me! In fact, I may fasten it to my clothing with a safety pin.

Waist pouches are made with slimmer people in mind, so I had to enlarge the waistband by inserting a piece of elastic. Unfortunately the only elastic I had was white, and the waistband is black, so I am going to be wandering around Russia with a constant reminder to one and all (not that they need one) that I am too fat. I also plan to put a third wad of bills into a plastic bag, and pin it inside a side pocket of my black pants, which are unfashionably baggy. Good thing I'm not the tights and miniskirt type; not much concealment there! I plan to wear a lot of black (my New York upbringing), in hopes of blending into the crowd. I'd rather look as little as possible like a moving target. Afraid I won't look Russian, though. Should I wear a babushka? No, it would drive me crazy to have something on my head all the time.

I bought some gifts to take along—useful things like food, stockings, hand cream etc.—not much, because of the weight. I'm hoping I can just give people American money. It's lightweight, and they need hard currency. Hope they won't be offended, though. This could get tricky.

Now I'm at the university. Joe is snoring on the sofa, exhausted from wrestling with the weird computer they have here. There was e-mail waiting from the Gomel physicist, who is being most helpful. I've never even met this man. How can I possibly repay him? He writes:

"Yes, Yasha Shnir is a good choice for being a guide! He is my very close friend and my colleague in Minsk. Actually, we work in the same institute and his office is next to mine. O.K., we really have some results. But there are a lot of unexpected problems always in Russia."

"Yasha." I like the sound of it better than "Yaakov Mikhailovich"—it sounds friendlier. But I'm concerned because we still haven't heard from him via e-mail, although we've sent him several messages. Time is getting short. Is he really willing to be my guide? Does he have a car? Can he find me a place to stay? I hope so, because I've cancelled my Intourist hotel reservation in Minsk; I'd much rather stay in a private flat, or with a family, and get an idea of what real life is like. I hope this wasn't a mistake.

Maybe this is what the Gomel physicist meant when he wrote, "there are a lot of unexpected problems always in Russia."

We haven't heard a word from Boris Ioffe in Moscow either. Have sent him details of my arrival time, but don't know if he's received them, or whether anyone is planning to meet me at the airport.

I'm off to the shops again. Only a couple more business days remain for me to take care of everything, as we are going to Goteborg tomorrow for three days. This is a trip I'd gladly do without, but since it seems to be very important to Joe that I go there with him, I'm going.

Oh, I'd almost forgotten my "ShtetlWorld" fantasy (probably should have)—that's ShtetlWorld as in Disneyworld. This is it: some enterprising Belarusian Jews should organize bed and breakfasts for American Jews who want to search out their roots (I can't be the only masochist in America, they'll be following in my footsteps once I've beaten a path, right?). And if there's nothing left to be seen, a little historical research followed by some construction and, voila! A reconstructed shtetl[2] to visit! Ethnic dancing, performances of *Fiddler on the Roof*, klezmer bands... And let's not forget the serious side, lectures on anti-Semitism, a Chernobyl video, encounter groups with former commissars, radioactive souvenirs in the gift shop... masses of hard currency flowing into the country.... I'm going off the deep end.

Sunday, August 16, 1992. Oh god, I'm leaving in two days, assuming the threatened strike by Russian air traffic controllers doesn't materialize. I've spoken to Yasha Shnir! He really exists! He has a heavy Russian accent and sounds sleepy, perhaps because I woke him up at six a.m., the only time I could get through to Minsk. He has a car and will meet me at the airport. I didn't get a feel for what he's like, but everyone says he's okay so I'll just have to hope they're right.

What's worrisome is that I still haven't heard a word from Boris Ioffe. I keep trying and trying to phone him, but it's absolutely impossible to get through to Moscow. What kind of an evil empire is this? What if I was trying to declare war, for god's sake?

We have sent a telex, which "should get there within forty-eight hours."

That's when I'm leaving, folks!

My fear is that Boris and Nina haven't received any of my e-mail. They may have no idea when (or if) I'm arriving, or that I've accepted their invitation to stay with them, either. Maybe they've gone on their vacation.

What if I arrive in Moscow without knowing a single soul there who speaks English and can't get a hotel room? What if I have to go crawling to Intourist and they spurn me?

Better keep trying to telephone Moscow.

Tomorrow I pick up my visa and tickets at the travel agency, finish my packing, and do a few last-minute errands.

---

2   Shtetl: *Yiddish for a small town or village*

Pernilla, my Overeaters Anonymous sponsor (yes, I've managed to find O.A. in Stockholm), advises me to take along an amulet of the Venus of Willendorf, since a vaguely pagan sense of connectedness to the Earth Mother, in no way a Jewish concept, is the best I can do to "keep in touch with my spirituality." They keep nagging you to do this in O.A. She says these chubby trinkets can be found at a shop in Gamla Stan, but I have no time to go there.

Poor old Earth Mother has been totally violated and desecrated in Belarus, from the sound of it. Forest fires, Chernobyl, the Nazi and Stalinist devastations—how can a spiritual connection there with Earth Mother be anything but profoundly sad? I don't want to experience the tragedies of the past, the sufferings of my own people, yet it's inevitable that I will. How can one possibly cling to Anne Frank's belief that people are really "good at heart"?

I've been collecting news items about Russia from the *Herald Tribune*. None of the news is good.

Wild mushrooms have caused a wave of poisonings in Belarus and Ukraine (600 ill and 60 dead in Ukraine alone). These mushrooms look exactly like edible species. There's speculation they may have mutated, due to radiation from Chernobyl. Another theory is that normally harmless mushrooms are drawing toxic substances from the soil for lack of moisture in a hot, dry summer. My theory: E. M. is losing her patience.

Garbage fires in Moscow have caused severe pollution, filling the air with bitter, yellow smoke.

Russian air traffic controllers will go on strike tomorrow if the government fails to meet demands over wages and other issues.

Russia plans to curb electricity 25% due to a shortage of energy resources. "General chaos and cuts in nuclear power have taken their toll."

August 17, 1992, 6 a.m. Leaving tomorrow morning, and I still haven't been able to reach Boris Ioffe by phone; so I still don't know if he'll be at the airport. And I don't know his address in Moscow.

I called Yasha Shnir again. He sounds nice. He'll meet me at the airport in Minsk and will keep trying to reach Ioffe. I asked if I could bring him anything special. "Oh no!

No!" He sounded shocked. I kept asking and he kept saying, "No." This makes me uneasy. I've been assuming we would reach some sort of business arrangement when I'm there, because I certainly want to compensate him for his time. I don't know him, it's not as if he were a friend. And he'll be squiring me around for days.

But what if he won't take money? I would feel terribly, uncomfortably in his debt. Why is he doing this, anyway? Does he hope Joe will help him professionally, if he one day comes to America? (Not unreasonable.) Is he doing Lev Okun a favor? Or is this simply Belarusian hospitality to a visiting American? If so, it's extreme. True, I've been hospitable to visiting Russians, not expecting anything in return; but not to this extent. I'd better tread carefully; I don't know the customs, and I don't want to offend by offering payment inappropriately.

Despite the remaining uncertainties, I am feeling calmer and no longer afraid. What will be, will be. I talked about my fears at an O.A. meeting last night, and it helped. After all, the worst thing that can happen is that I'll die. Well, we all have to die sometime, and I've had a wonderfully full life.

I continue to feel I was destined to make this trip.

I spoke to my cousin Lois yesterday. She called some of the relatives, but learned little. The most interesting bit of information about Streshin was that in 1895—just the period I want to write about—it contained 1300 Jews and 500 non-Jews. She also told me Shirley Yaeger died six months ago. That strident, angry voice stilled. Another person gone who knew my mother.

Later. Nerves aplenty as the day wears on, for we have not reached Boris by phone, and someone at the Moscow Institute where he works kindly sent Joe an e-mail message to let him know that none of our messages over the last two weeks have gotten through, due to a malfunction in their computers. This means Boris and Nina do not know I'm arriving tomorrow.

Panic time. Better left undescribed.

At four o'clock I picked up my visa and ticket at the travel agency. No problem.
Came home, phone was ringing—Joe got a message from Boris—yay! All systems are
down (as if we didn't know), but he will meet Dorothy at the airport tomorrow and take
her to Nina's daughter's apartment. Euphoria!

Tomorrow I'm off! And I got through the whole day without a chocolate bar, even
though there are four in my suitcase, for gifts.

II. Moscow

August 19, 1992, Moscow, Boris and Nina Ioffe's apartment. On my arrival at Sheremetyevo airport, I was detained by Passport Control. Evidently my passport and visa were in order, but something, some third document, was missing. Sternly, the militiaman kept demanding it in Russian mixed with a few words of English, too few for me to understand him. I kept pulling papers from my purse—the receipt from the travel agency, my tickets, the hotel reservation for my last night in Russia—and inquiring hopefully, "Is this it? Is this it?"

"Nyet! Nyet!"

I had a hunch he was looking for an itinerary from Intourist, an official list of where I would be spending each night; the Russian embassy in Stockholm had told me I would need one before they could issue me a visa. Of course I had no such document, because the travel agency had somehow obtained the visa for me after I'd paid them thirty dollars in Swedish kroner. It didn't seem wise to mention this. "I'm staying with friends," I kept repeating. "They're meeting me at the airport."

"Nyet! Nyet!"

He summoned another officer and they conferred, frowning. The second man shuffled through my papers, and when he came to the receipt from the travel agency, which happened to specialize in trips from Stockholm to Israel, raised his head, gave me a cold stare, and said, "Israel." He resumed shuffling, and the charade went on. I kept smiling and nodding, trying to look as idiotic as possible. "Could this be it? I'm terribly sorry to be such a nuisance." I hauled out more papers. "Maybe these?"

The officers exchanged looks of intense annoyance. The second officer leaned forward, narrowing his eyes and searching my face to see if I resembled one of the "Wanted" posters at KGB headquarters. Finally he shrugged and barked, "Go!"

Before he could change his mind, I trotted off with a friendly wave.

According to the last-minute telex I'd received, Boris Ioffe was to meet me at the airport. I hoped I would recognize him. We'd met in America a few months earlier, but I recalled him only vaguely. I looked around for a small, gray man; quite a few were to be seen. Then one detached himself from a wall and came toward me, tentatively. He had thinning gray hair, a narrow, pessimistic face, and beetling black eyebrows. The eyebrows looked familiar. I moved in his direction.

"Dorothy?"

"Boris! I'm so glad to see you! I thought I was going to be arrested!"

"I was not sure it was you. Arrested?" He seized the handle of my luggage cart and began to drag it along, scraping the bottom loudly against the floor.

"I think you have to slant it—"

He ignored me. "We must find a taxi." He took off, wrestling the cart ahead of him and grinding the base into the cement so that it offered maximum resistance.

"Actually, it's better if you pull it—"

"We must look for a taxi with a meter. The private taxis are not safe, especially for tourists. If you ever have to take a taxi, you must be extremely careful." We came to a curb, which he took at top speed. The cart stuck and then plunged over the brink. The bags fell off. Impatiently, he pushed them back on.

"If you just back it over—"

"The taxi queue is there." He sped up, grinding the cart ahead of him.

I reminded myself that, although a brilliant man, Boris was a theoretical physicist; managing a luggage cart evidently fell into the realm of the experimental. I could tell he was too macho to let me take the cart from him. Trailing after him, I resigned myself.

After much bargaining he selected a taxi. We sped off toward Moscow while he told me with disgust that the taxi driver had refused to accept less than twenty dollars, a sizeable percentage of Boris's monthly salary. "Oh, but I'll pay for it," I said. "I insist. It's great that you met me at the airport, really, but please don't even think about the cab."

"No, no," he said, but perfunctorily, and changed the subject. We were heading for the flat of Nina's daughter, he informed me, which Nina was cleaning in readiness for my arrival.

"But I'd much rather stay with you and Nina," I said. In a telex some weeks earlier, he'd offered me my choice of either place, perhaps an impulse he'd later regretted. I decided to ignore that possibility.

"But we live out in the suburbs," he protested. "Nina's daughter is presently at the dacha with her family, and you could have her flat to yourself. I think that would be better. It is only twenty minutes from downtown."

It made sense, but the prospect of finding myself all alone in Moscow was too daunting. My brush with Passport Control had done nothing to change my feeling that Russia was a frightening country. "I don't mind being in the suburbs," I said. "I'll come in on the subway."

He looked at me to see if I was serious. "Alone?"

I swallowed. "Certainly, alone."

He sighed and accepted the inevitable.

We picked up Nina, who appeared very sweaty and red in the face, and was lugging cleaning supplies.

"Aren't you terribly hot?" she greeted me. I was wearing a long-sleeved shirt and a jacket, and Moscow was indeed very hot and muggy.

"Yes!" I exclaimed as we embraced. "Nina, it's so good to see you!" I had liked this strong, opinionated woman when we'd met in Maryland last winter. We'd gone together to an indoor swimming pool.

"So you are staying with us! And I have cleaned my daughter's apartment for nothing. For her I would not do it!"

"Tell her now she has to clean your apartment," I said, and she laughed.

As Nina prepared dinner, Boris invited me to sit down with him at the living room table, a ritual I would come to know well.

"Now," he said, folding his hands. "Tell me why you have come to Russia, and what you hope to accomplish here." His manner was diffident, his narrow shoulders stooped in a self-effacing way, but there was a steely glint under the bushy eyebrows. I could see he was considering me for the first time, like a physics problem. In America he hadn't particularly noticed me—nor I him, for that matter.

I didn't really know what to say. Why was I here? This wasn't my kind of trip at all. I'm fat and I loathe discomfort. I'm lazy, a worrier, I never walk when I can take the car, and I have plenty of middle-aged aches and pains. A fantasy about Russia was one thing, but how to explain the fact that I was actually here—not just to him but to myself? Was it Destiny, whatever that meant? Somehow, and quite strongly, I felt this to be the case, although I couldn't imagine why Destiny should bother about me. Yet, everything had unrolled so quickly and easily. All the obstacles, and there had been many, had melted away until, without ever making a conscious decision, I realized that I was actually going to make the trip. Maybe Fate had somebody else in mind and I just an instrument, my visit a stone dropped into a pond. Who could tell where the ripples would wash up?

I am not a mystic. All my life I've thought of myself as a practical person. Could I confess these irrational notions to Boris, who was waiting for an answer with all the patience of a cat at a mouse hole? No. Instead I said I'd been thinking about writing a historical novel based on the life of my grandfather, who had come from a village called Streshin. I felt I should visit Russia to get a picture of what Jewish life might have been like in Belarus at the turn of the century. I wanted to visit Streshin.

For some time now I'd been using this explanation whenever the question came up. It was even true; yet I always felt fraudulent when I produced it, and surprised that people accepted it when it was so far from the whole truth. Certainly I was a writer; I'd published two novels in the past four years, and was working on a third, but they were mysteries, mere light entertainments. I wasn't at all sure I could write a historical novel. Research, the kind you did in books, was something I'd never cared for, though I did like going places to soak up an atmosphere, and talking to people who knew things I didn't. And I had major doubts that I could write a serious book. Humor was always creeping into my writing, no matter how I tried to keep it out. I didn't know if I was capable of writing about pogroms, and starvation, and the slaughter of innocent people; or if I really wanted to. I didn't know if I still had the energy, or the necessary ambition, to carry out a project with a certain epic sweep. I didn't know if I had enough years left—I was fifty-nine. Not that one ever knows, at any age.

These things went through my mind whenever someone asked me, as Boris had just done, why I wanted to go to Russia. Sure I'd like to write a book about my grandfather, but most likely the task was beyond me. So I was always careful to say that I'd "thought" of writing such a book, not that I "intended" to. Of course actions start in thoughts, or rather in daydreams and fantasies; so it was possible that, just as I'd once "thought" of going to Russia, and now was actually here, I might one day write "THE END" on the last page of a book about my grandfather—a daunting notion, which I pushed away.

Boris was saying, "I have never heard of Streshin. Are you sure it still exists?"

This was a possibility that hadn't occurred to me. "But why wouldn't it?"

He shook his head as if shocked at the depths of my ignorance. "Belarus was in the

Bundists of 1903. Max Hankin seated second from left.

Pale of Jewish settlement. It suffered greatly during World War II, and many villages were completely destroyed. The Nazis killed all the people and burned down the houses."

"I guess I sort of knew that, but—" My uncertainties about Streshin had, until now, centered on the question of whether it really was the town my grandfather had come from. I mistrusted my childhood memories, and most of the relatives I'd consulted had seemed uncertain. The only reference to Streshin I'd come upon in the family papers was a yellowed photograph someone had clipped from the *Jewish Daily Forward*. "An interesting group of Bundists, Streshin, 1903," said the caption, followed by a few lines of Yiddish I was unable to read. My grandfather, age nineteen, sat in the first row with his legs crossed, wearing a moustache and a natty suit, and holding an elegant cane. Since the grandfather I'd known had been clean-shaven, profoundly indifferent to politics, and given to wearing paint-splattered overalls, this picture with its hint of an earlier existence and, conceivably, hidden depths to his character had always intrigued me. It didn't prove he came from Streshin, though, only that he'd been there when the picture was taken. Now I considered the possibility that Streshin no longer existed. It was a disorienting thought. Some part of me, so small it was hardly there at all, or so I had assumed, was tethered to this almost mythical shtetl in Belarus, like a boat on a very long anchor chain. Had I come this far to find—nothing? A void instead of a village? I said, "It's on the map. I've seen the name, in very small letters, near a city called Gomel."

"The fires?" He nodded, surprised I'd heard about them. I told him there had been an item in the Swedish press that said the drought had caused fires in the forests and in the peat moss. The latter, which had absorbed much of the radioactivity from the nuclear accident, was now releasing it into the air.

"All right, then you know about it. You'll only be there a short time, I don't think there's much danger." He rose and went to the bookcase. "Streshin—let us see if we can look it up. I assume it was a Jewish town—"

"Apparently it had 1300 Jews in 1895, and 500 non-Jews."

"Oh, you know all about it."

"No, no. One of my cousins told me she'd heard that from a distant relative, who thought he'd heard it a long time ago from his father. It's all I know. It may not even be true."

He began to take down books. "It so happens I have a Jewish encyclopedia, about a hundred years old. I bought it second hand, and some of the volumes are missing. But maybe we can find Streshin."

"That would be great!" I said. Streshin, in a book! Actual, factual information! And the date couldn't be more perfect—my grandfather had been born in 1884, and left for America in 1905.

Boris searched along the shelf behind the books he'd removed, where there was a second, inner row. To save space, or for concealment, I wondered? Boris was Jewish, of course. He made an irritated little noise. "Tsk. I don't have the volume."

"Oh, too bad!" I said, feeling let down. "Oh well. Maybe we could look up Gomel."

"If I have the volume— Here it is." He brought it over to the table, adjusted his glasses, and read for a few minutes in silence. Then he pushed the book away. "When this was published, the city had 37,000 people, mostly Jewish. In the uyest, which is like a district or province, the population was 228,000. Gomel is a very old city, older than Moscow. It says here it was founded in 1142. It belonged to the Duke of Chernigov, who lived in Kiev. There was a very big pogrom in the seventeenth century, and Cossacks killed two thousand to ten thousand Jews."

"Ten thousand?" He nodded. "What do you mean, 'two thousand to ten thousand'?"

"The exact number isn't known." Two to ten thousand. I hadn't conceived of pogroms that massive. I'd imagined three or four days to a week of rioting and property damage, with widespread beatings and isolated incidents of murder and rape, something like a race riot in America.

This was on a different scale.

Nina appeared at the door of the living room, and stuck her head inside. "Dinner is ready, do you want to wash your hands?"

"We must eat now," said Boris, and stood up. "We can look at the books again later, if you like."

Later: Notes from Boris's books, a 1902 Russian encyclopedia and a turn of the century Jewish encyclopedia.

> **GOMEL: 1902 -** Trial of Jews who had refused for two years to pay a special tax. They were given a penalty.
>
> In 1766, 359 Jews.
>
> 1897: 20,700 Jews in Gomel; many tailors; trade in farm goods.
>
> 2 Talmud Torah schools for boys - HS.
>
> 1 had manual training
>
> 2 gen. girls
>
> 1 girls' "professional" school
>
> County seat of district; administrative.

BORIS'S MEMORIES. In 1933, when he was eight or so, Boris and his mother spent nine months in a shtetl with his grandmother, after his grandfather's death. He recalled a big cobblestone square with two-story buildings around it containing small shops: a grocer, photographer, fishmonger, and butcher. Nearby were the synagogue and cheder. At Succoth, his grandmother built a sukkah in the courtyard. Jewish and Polish children played together and relations as he remembers them were good. On the Sabbath a Polish girl would come in to light the fire.

Yeshiva buchers[1] were respected and it was considered a blessing to put one up free of charge. Boris remembers such a young man, who had his own corner in the big room, with his bed. He always wore a hat; the first thing in the morning, he put on his hat, while wearing his underclothes.

Everyone slept in the same room on wooden beds, under woven covers.

On Friday his grandmother cooked meat and potatoes with prunes; these were kept warm in the floor-to-ceiling clay heating stove until Saturday night. Boris slept with his mother.

Customs were strong, and most of the Jews were very religious. There were a few "liberals," like the doctor. At eight and coming from Moscow, Boris was a skeptic. He remembers old men used to stop him on the street and say, "So, Boris, is there a God?"

"No!" he would say, and they would look worried.

He showed me a coverlet (probably for a table) from his grandmother's house, made of heavy linen, almost as heavy as wool, and woven of dark green and pale yellowish fibers. I looked at it a long time, imagining a child fingering it as he was falling asleep. Dark green, blackish, like the shadowy depths of the pinewoods. Creamy white, like the skin of a pale girl. Or the fields when the hay has been cut. He played with a tassel at the corner, ran a finger along the Greek key design of the border. In each of the four corners, a pair of horns spilled green and white flowers. He would count the flowers and then the leaves as he fell asleep. On the reverse the green mostly vanished, mysteriously. Where did it go? A few ghostly shapes in the creamy background, of the horns in reverse. All the flowers had vanished.

---

1   *Apprentices in rabbinic schools at the times of Tsarist Russia.*

MAPS. It is hard to find a map of Moscow, not accidentally. Boris told me someone was awarded the Stalin Prize for coming up with a formula for creating a deliberately inaccurate map—a non-negligible problem. What he did was draw wavy horizontal and vertical lines across the map and then he "pulled them straight," distorting all the adjacent surface features.

BIG AND SMALL SCIENCE. From the taxi Boris pointed out a low building, the Landau Institute, and the nearby Academy of Sciences building, a towering monolith so costly it still isn't paid for. He said, "Small building, big science; big building—no science at all!"

August 19, 1992. I've been in Russia now for a little more than a day. It's eleven o'clock and I'm in bed, on the sofa in Nina's study, which also serves as a guest room for Boris's son, who lives in Rutgers. Earlier today, near Red Square, I took the pedestrian underpass beneath Okhotny Ryad and an enormous, open square—it's impossible to cross them on the surface, which means one is walking up and down stairs continually. Not easy for people with any sort of difficulty walking, including myself due to mild arthritis. But little about Russia is designed to spare the weak. In the late afternoon, tired from sightseeing and the impossibility of finding any place to sit down, I fell (forward, fortunately), as I reached the top of one of those stairs, and went sprawling on the pavement. People were streaming past me but nobody stopped to help me up or ask if I was all right. I knew I wasn't badly hurt—just a bruised knee—but it reminded me that I must always be extremely careful on stairs and pay attention to each step. I mustn't let my thoughts wander off, which they'd been doing at that moment.

The underground passages are very long and narrow, with tiled walls that were originally white but are now grimy and greasy, like all of Moscow I've seen so far except for the area immediately around the Kremlin and Red Square. The warm, fuggy atmosphere of the passage was welcome after the cold wind and rain aboveground, even though it smelled heavily of tobacco smoke. It was a lively enough scene, with crowds rushing in both directions. Two musicians played Russian songs, rather melancholy and soothing, on a guitar and a balalaika—I put a few rubles in their hat—and a few steps further a small combo was churning out execrable jazz. Every few paces some hopeful entrepreneur was trying to make a few rubles selling ice cream cones from a couple of cardboard boxes packed with dry ice, the fumes rising, or books, or pages from a stamp collection. There were a few beggars, not many—one old woman bent double, crossing herself ceaselessly as she stared down at the filthy floor, others sitting on the ground, between their outstretched legs cardboard placards containing their life stories, none of which I could read because they were in Russian. There was a holy picture displayed atop a cardboard carton. Before it a candle burned beside what looked like a glass fish tank containing a few crumpled rubles. One man was hawking girly posters from a folding table, before a sample display taped to the wall.

The level of sheer physical discomfort in Moscow is incredible. There are few benches, even in the well-kept strip of parkland bordering the Kremlin wall, and although I walked for a couple of hours around some of the main tourist attractions in downtown Moscow, around Red Square, there wasn't a single cafe or restaurant to be seen where one could sit down and have a cup of tea. There were a very few kiosks where a man had made a few open-face salami sandwiches, that sort of thing, but nothing inviting. Nowhere to sit down. It was extraordinary. The people of Moscow must be bone-weary all the time, a level of tiredness that is hard to grasp. All that queuing for food, running from one little shop to another in hopes that something you need will be in stock that day, or even something you don't need but might conceivably need in the future; having to do every trivial errand twice and three times over because all services are so inefficient. As Nina said in exasperation, "No one is responsible for anything!"

The information woman in the Lenin museum told me, when I asked her, about a cafe across the road which could be reached by means of the underground passage. I followed her directions, entered a side door of the vast, faceless Hotel Moskva, saw no cafe, but noticed an inconspicuous sign with a logo of a coffee cup in which some unknown hand had drawn a skull and crossbones in red marker. Climbing a few steps, I entered a dingy cafe containing not a single chair, just a dozen imitation-wood stand-up tables of surpassing ugliness in a columned marble chamber that looked as if it had wandered off from a hotel lobby sometime in the past and never found its way back. Unwashed windows overlooking the square, a cafeteria line, and a stern-looking cashier completed the scene.

I grabbed a tray with edges that seemed to have been attacked by a school of piranhas (all the trays were in the same condition), helped myself to bread and cheese, and looked in vain for a tea-dispensing machine. There were odds and ends of hot food—disintegrating chicken and watery vegetables. A woman in a white uniform appeared from the kitchen and slopped down a tray containing four bowls of soup. I decided to take one, since I'd been walking in the rain and wanted something hot. My chances seemed good, as there were only three people ahead of me; but alas, the first two each took a bowl and the third took two, leaving none for me.

I studied two groups of glasses containing unknown fluids. I touched a sample glass in the first glass. It was vaguely cool. A glass in the second group seemed vaguely hot, so I took it although it was gummy to the touch. I paid about 20 rubles, or a dime, for this meal of bread and cheese and a drink. Grateful to take some of the weight off my feet, I propped my elbows on a stand-up table and ate. The fluid turned out to be coffee, heavily presweetened; and although I am supposed to avoid sugar, I decided I'd better drink it. The dreariness of this cafe was overwhelming and made me understand why the McDonald's in Moscow is so wildly popular. If this is what people are used to, the mere idea of sitting down at a table in a clean, shiny, colorful environment and receiving food from people who have been trained to smile and be pleasant must be sheer heaven. I'd have been ecstatic if I'd found a McDonald's today! In fact it wasn't many blocks away, but I didn't see it.

After the cafe I walked down the avenue and stopped in a Christian Dior boutique, curious to see what the much-touted "new Russia" was like. The shop was deliciously fragrant, crowded with sparkling glass display cases filled with perfumes and cosmetics. People thronged in and out; I don't know how many actually bought anything, but a few of the women were fashionably dressed and looked like customers. Who these people were and how they got their money, I don't know. As I headed for the street through a small entrance foyer I noticed a woman holding a shopping bag full of perfumes, which some of the passersby paused to examine and then buy; I assumed these were black market items at a knocked-down price.

Half a block further along, a queue waited patiently outside the dazzlingly white plastic storefront of a Dannon yogurt shop. I don't know whether this was plain or frozen yogurt. It might have been either. The Ioffes had told me yogurt was hard to get in Moscow; I was surprised, having assumed it was a staple food of the Russians. Maybe I confused it with sour cream.

I stepped inside an upscale shop that sold better-quality Russian crafts and pottery, priced in rubles. They were not cheap. They had a lot of the blue and white Russian porcelain Nina Ioffe collects; it can be rather charming. She gave me a vase as a gift. There was jewelry, painted woodenware, the inevitable matrioschka dolls, and Palekh boxes. A miscellany of other objects: sheaves of fiber optics spilling out of vases, kitschy odds and ends. The store was mobbed with people, most of them looking and not buying. All the people who'd been absent from the cavernous halls of the Lenin museum seemed to be here.

On the next block I went inside a shop that sold meat and cheese. Here there were long queues, and an atmosphere of desperation yet determination emanated from the people, mostly women, who stood there with bags dangling from their fists as the line inched forward, their feet no doubt aching.

These were the fancy downtown stores—not impressive, except as compared with the Ioffe's neighborhood grocery store, which I visited this morning. Ioffe had just wanted to stop in and see whether they had any of "the good milk" today, but in fact they had no milk at all. This was a filthy, battered, dimly-lit small shop; as soon as you walked through the door you were struck by the stench of putrefaction. There were a few sausages in the cases and not much else. Outside the door, an elderly woman stood with a few bags of plums on the ground. Boris explained that she was a private seller, and perhaps the plums came from her own tree. This is newly legal. Many small kiosks have recently sprung up, especially near the subway stops. Some are former newspaper kiosks, stolen at night or when the proprietors were away on vacation, and resold to hopeful new entrepreneurs. Nina Ioffe said, "You can buy anything you want in Moscow now, anything. If you have the money." For many people these things are unobtainable, and for most it entails some sacrifice to afford fresh fruit or vegetables. I have been enjoying the Russian rye bread, which is very cheap by American standards at six rubles a loaf (up a ruble since last month), and I had a couple of slices with butter and cheese, and a cup of tea, when I got back to the Ioffes' apartment after my excursion to Moscow.

I felt very tense, heading downtown on the subway to the Kremlin, on my own in Moscow for the first time. To be unable to read the Russian alphabet with any fluency is an enormous handicap; still, even the minimal knowledge of it I've managed to scrape up is helpful, and I did manage to get off at the right stop, and to return home without mishap. I followed Boris's excruciatingly detailed instructions, pausing now and then to consult the diagrams he'd drawn in my pocket notebook.

In the Lenin Museum, August 19. This is an incredible experience and I'm so glad I came—and spending the day alone in Moscow is better in a way than if I had a guide/companion as a buffer.

It is raining. The Kremlin, I discovered after much walking to reach the entrance, is closed today because it is the one-year anniversary of the coup; it will remain closed during my three days in Moscow. I trudged back toward Red Square and bought a pack of unlovely postcards from a boy of twelve or so, for a dollar, because I felt sorry for him. Took refuge in the Lenin Museum, where I am now. Silent, echoing, near-empty halls. Boring exhibits. Vast canvases on the walls thronged with crowds of people, eager workers listening to Lenin's oratory in every conceivable setting. But as for flesh-and-blood people, no one is here, even on a rainy day.

I had a pleasant conversation with an information lady whose English was quite good. She kept telling me of wonderful museums I should visit (not this one), only a few subway stops away, ignoring my protests that I wanted to stay within walking distance of Teatralnaya stop so I could find my way home. Whenever my eyes drifted away she would rap out, "Pay attention!"—but in a friendly way. After the third or fourth "Pay attention" she told me there was a wonderful glass exhibition on the third floor. Yes, of this building. Yes, the Lenin museum.

I took what seemed like many escalators upstairs, because the floors were broken up confusingly into half-floors. Asked directions of a dumpy, deeply depressed woman seated on a hard chair, who stared at me with dead eyes when I asked if she spoke English, and did not reply. I tried again: "Where is the glass exhibit? Glass? Exhibit?"

"Russian," she said, stony-faced.

"Oh, you speak only Russian."

"Russian."

At the entrance to the glass exhibit, a slightly older lady smilingly played charades with me until I figured out I had to buy a ticket, and did so for five rubles (about five cents). Without a word of English, she managed to project playfulness and charm.

On display were spun and blown glass pieces, mostly botanical, by a single artist. They were a welcome antidote to the Moscow I'd seen so far, which brings to mind a thick, muddy boot trampling everything in sight. A heavy layer of grime seems to cover all of Moscow, but these delicate objects, of no practical utility whatsoever, were fragile, fanciful, and sparkling clean. What a joy it was to see them! Tears came to my eyes, and I forgave the traces of kitsch.

I have been sitting for half an hour in the Lenin Museum library before a mute TV set, writing. Suddenly people appear, and an ancient lady in a black dress switches on the set. A film begins. It shows Lenin's funeral cortege. Do these people worship death? Feebly, the ancient lady delivers a commentary in Russian. The corpse appears, the important mourners are named—behind me, a voice breathes, "Karenin"—and the film is over.

Boris took me to the bank this morning to change some dollars into rubles. We were turned away. The people at the bank didn't know the exchange rate. They said, "Maybe this afternoon." He loaned me 2,000 rubles (about $18), and was worried about my flashing this wad around town. He was relieved when I told him all the various places about my person I stowed it.

I've never talked as much about money in my life as since I came to Russia—twenty-two hours ago, now. Paranoia is everywhere. I'm nervous of talking to strangers. Both Boris and Nina have warned me several times not to have my money stolen. I expressed an interest in buying a Palekh box and Nina said, "But they are enormously expensive now, enor-r-rmously expensive!"

"How much?"

"Two thousand rubles."

Eighteen dollars.

Nina said she reads only mysteries now. "We have some very good writers in Russia—yes, even now—but I do not read them. It is too—what do you say in English?"

"Depressing?"

"Yes, depressing."

"Too much like real life?"

"Yes—of course real life!"

Nina is making piroshky in the kitchen as I dictate. I can hear her chopping. It is almost midnight. I'm not as tired as I might be, because I had a nap earlier. The canned ham I brought is being incorporated into the piroshky. The chocolate mints from the duty-free shop at the airport were also well received, especially by Boris, who ceremoniously unwraps a few and eats them after each meal, even though he confided in me that he is not fond of mint because it reminds him of toothpaste. He also liked the copy of the *New York Times* in Russian, which I bought from a subway hawker today to take back to Joe, who loves the *Times*. Boris, though, had never seen this publication before, and has made off with it.

Boris, Nina, and I had a long talk tonight about the intricacies of Soviet scientific politics in the Academy of Sciences. It was quite depressing. He feels anti-Semitism is increasing. Since the breakup of the Soviet Union there has been a movement, a successful one, to "Russianize" the sciences. I naively assumed this meant electing members who lived in Russia rather than one of the other republics, but in fact it means electing academicians with Russian surnames. Those whose names sound Jewish, Moslem, etc. have been ousted.

Also, a number of politicians who aren't scientists at all have been elected, because they wanted to be Academicians! "Why?" I asked. "The prestige?"

"The power. The salary, the car, the dacha."

Boris explained that at his institute, perhaps the best in Moscow, there is only one computer used by the entire staff for sending e-mail messages, a vital link with the outside world since the telephone system is so unsatisfactory. This computer is prone to intermittent breakdown. "This is why I always send only short messages. Just business. If I try to send a long message and the machine breaks down in the middle, I lose the whole message and must start again. If I send a short message I lower the probability that it will be interrupted."

Everyone must stand in line and wait in turn to receive their e-mail.

It looks as though they may lose even the one e-mail hookup they have, he said. I found this shocking and hard to believe. But there is only one private company, a monopoly that runs the e-mail and charges a fee for carrying the messages to the borders of Russia. From that point, a German network picks up the cost of relaying them to their final destination. The Russian monopoly has just informed the Institute that in six months they are going to have to pay six million rubles for six months of domestic e-mail service, money they do not have. There is no way to negotiate or find another carrier. Nor does the company care at all if the Institute drops the service, since plenty of other would-be customers are lined up and waiting.

Tomorrow Boris and I will go to the bank again and try to change some money. He says I could get a better rate on the black market, perhaps ten percent more, but he's afraid to do it because he feels these people are untrustworthy, perhaps even dangerous. They might hand you a thick wad of bills that is padded with worthless paper in the middle. Or they might even have a confederate who would follow you, hit you over the head, and steal the money. The bank, he says, is safer. That's fine with me.

Boris says I will get so many rubles for a hundred dollars—which we decided is what I should exchange—that I'll need a large bag to hold them. He's planning to take a zippered canvas bag about a foot square. The government has banned 50-ruble and 100-ruble notes in a futile attempt to control the black market, but has only managed to complicate further the lives of ordinary citizens. A hundred dollars is sixteen thousand rubles—a fortune, compared to a Russian salary. Threading my way today through the vendors around Red Square, I saw a boy of about fifteen who had been hawking postcards approach a couple of his friends. He was waving a five-ruble note; then with a flourish he pressed it to his lips and kissed it. Five rubles are worth less than a nickel.

Yasha Shnir, who is to be my guide and translator in Belarus, called tonight to ask Boris the Russian names of my relatives. Yasha has found a Jewish society in Minsk with burial records that go back 200 years, and is trying to find out where my great-grandmother, Esther Basia, is buried. Also he has offered me his flat for the two nights I'll be in Minsk.

Boris said, "He asked what to do about food for you. I told him frankly not to worry, you were a very independent lady, and you have money." He added, "You should know that these people in Minsk are probably just on the border of actual hunger."

Thursday night, August 20, 1992. Boris says bitterly, "Every day we have to fight to survive." He was on the telephone at 10:30 this evening trying to get through to a taxi company so he could order a cab to take me to the airport tomorrow. He'd assured me there would be no problem. If we called the day before, the taxi would come.

When after many attempts he finally got through, he was told that to order a taxi in his district he would have to call another number the following morning. But Nina refused to accept this, and she and Boris have been trying for over an hour now to reach a taxi company (there are several); the lines are continually busy, or nobody answers. This is making me very uneasy, as my plane leaves for Minsk tomorrow afternoon, and I'm afraid I may miss my plane. I also feel guilty about wasting so much of the Ioffes' time, although there is nothing I can do about it. As I don't speak Russian, I can't call the cab myself.

I said, "What is the suicide rate in Russia? This kind of thing must make people very depressed."

Boris said, "This information is not available. But I can tell you that the mortality rate is now higher than the birth rate. In a civilized country this is unheard of. People aren't having children."

Nina said, "To raise a child is hard here. Who can afford the fruit, the vegetables, a child needs? The meat! I have a friend who is an obstetrician, a very good one. One patient came to her, she has two children already and was pregnant with the third. My friend said to her, 'You are going to have it? You will have three children? Are you crazy?' Yes, a doctor said this!"

We sat around gloomily a while longer, until Nina told me, "Dorothy, go to bed, you look very tiresome."

I burst out laughing. When I explained what "tiresome" meant, we all laughed companionably.

Boris has just popped his head into my room to say he got through and was told there is absolutely nothing he can do tonight. He'll suspend his efforts, everybody will go to bed, and at nine in the morning he'll start again.

I'd been planning a quick return trip to the Old Arbat tomorrow to buy gifts to take home; but if necessary, of course, I'll simply stay here and take any taxi I can get. Or resort to public transportation, a four-hour trip.

It's really incredible how disorganized this country is, and how the people survive this continual frustration, delay, wasted time, and physical exhaustion.

August 21, 1992, 7 a.m., the Ioffes' apartment, Moscow. Wondering how I will get to the airport for my flight to Minsk. Wondering how incredibly difficult it may be to fly out of Gomel. Yasha Shnir told me several times, "Minsk is better." But by then the travel agent couldn't change my reservation.

Last night Boris didn't come home from work until nearly 10 o'clock. Nina was annoyed because "He never telephones!" Probably telephoning is as difficult as everything else around here. I stayed in my room, reading. I figured the Ioffes could use a little time alone. Boris, especially, "Never wants to invite anyone over," according to Nina. But to my surprise he knocked on my door and invited me to join him in the kitchen while he had his supper.

He told me he was talking to the Assistant Director of the Institute for two and a half hours, about the financial crisis. They want to try and set up a joint project with Los Alamos, which has fallen on hard times in these post-Cold-War days. "The Assistant Director is quite good, but the Chief Director is very bad, unfortunately. Probably he will not approve this plan. Most of the time we talked about how to go around him.

"In the Cold War, there was more support. In the U. S. they would say, 'Oh, the Russians have it, they are ahead of us!' Then they would get support. Of course, if the Russians have it, the U. S. must have it too. And here it was always, "The Americans have it!" So we would get support." As he was finishing his supper he said, "By the way, I received a message from Joe."

"By the way? You didn't tell me that first?"

"It was nothing important. He sends you a kiss."

Afterwards, on the evening news, sandwiched between scenes of fighting in Georgia and Bosnia, and a beaming Yeltsin greeting the Olympic athletes, there was a very brief item about Chernobyl, maybe two sentences.

I said, "What was that about Chernobyl?"

Boris said, "He says it is safe."

"Safe? What does he mean?"

He shrugged. "He says it is safe. That is all."

CHANGING MONEY; THE OLD ARBAT. Boris went to the bank for the second time this morning to try and change my money; he was again told, "Impossible." Yesterday they didn't know the exchange rate. Today they didn't have any money.

Therefore, Nina agreed with some trepidation to change my money on the black market. They needed to change some dollars too, for their vacation trip next week. I handed her the vast sum of forty dollars—four ten dollar bills—and we took the subway down to the Arbat.

There we browsed the tables of the vendors, which were set up in rows all down the middle of the street for several blocks, like a vast flea market. All these private enterprises have sprung up since Gorbachev—before, they were illegal—and most of the sellers are young, sometimes very young, men. There were plenty of customers, most of whom spoke Russian, though I heard English a few times. We examined the painted wooden Palekh ware, comparing prices, and Nina would ask the vendors rather disdainfully, "Is this real Palekh, or imitation?" Sometimes it was one, sometimes the other.

Then she suddenly said, "Wait here," and went up to the window of a large kiosk that seemed to be selling soft drinks and cigarettes, knocked on the glass, and spoke in a low voice to the man inside. A moment later he came out a side door and ushered her through. They vanished, and the door closed after them. I realized she must be changing the money.

I loitered at the nearby tables, fending off aggressive salesmen and trying to look inconspicuous. It started to rain and I opened my umbrella as the vendors flung sheets of plastic over their wares. Ten minutes passed. I didn't want to wander too far in the crowds for fear we would miss each other when she emerged.

When she'd been inside fifteen minutes, I saw a uniformed militiaman march up to the kiosk. "Oh no!" I thought. He gave one knock, pulled the door open, and went inside. I thought, "Oh my god, she's going to be arrested. What do I do now? This is a disaster!" Apprehensively I waited. Nothing happened. She wasn't dragged out in handcuffs.

After a while the militiaman reappeared. He strolled off. More time passed.

Finally she emerged, clutching her bulging pocketbook and beaming. When she caught sight of me she hurried over and opened her bag to show me it was stuffed full of bills.

"Close it!" I said, looking around nervously.

She told me the militiaman was a part of the black market operation, providing protection in exchange, no doubt, for a percentage of the profits. She said she, too, had been afraid when he'd entered the kiosk; then she realized his presence made the transaction safer, for it meant she wouldn't be cheated or knocked on the head.

Now we had money and could shop. I also had some dollars in my waist pouch. I decided to buy a painted wooden box, but now the question was how to transfer some of the money from Nina's purse to me in this dense crowd, without attracting undesirable attention. We walked for a block without finding a good place. I suggested a deserted side yard shielded by a couple of trucks and a dumpster, but Nina rejected it. Too empty. Dangerous gangs of youths sometimes lurked in such places.

Leaving the Arbat, we walked down a residential street. Halfway down the block a tunnel ran beneath an apartment building to the next street. I said, "How about this? We could just step inside."

She shook her head. "No, no, no, I am afraid. There must be people." She peered down the block. "Ah! You see that playground? It is perfect. We will sit quietly on a bench and count out your money."

The playground was large and wooded, and surrounded on three sides by apartment buildings. Children played on swings and slides while a few mothers chatted on benches. We made our way to the most secluded bench, carefully avoiding a man who stood swaying and drinking from a bottle.

For my forty dollars I had received 6800 rubles, all in twenty-five, five, or one-ruble notes. This was a great many rubles to count, and doing so made me nervous. Then there was the problem of how to dispose of them about my person, but fortunately the pants I was wearing had two roomy side pockets, and there was room for a wad in my waist pouch as well.

Well-padded under my loose black jacket, I fared forth and bought an amber ring for my daughter Anne for seven dollars, a round, black and red Palekh box for my cousin Edythe for twelve, several Palekh pictures, one for me and one for my son Anatol, and a round Palekh pin with a flower design, which I'm now wearing on my shirt. In addition I bought two small, whimsical pottery pieces. One, a kind of painted terra-cotta called Dimka ware, is a jaunty little turkey; the other, of blue-and-white Russian porcelain, is a bundled-up couple riding in a droshky pulled by three horses. Both of these will fit nicely into my collection of small animals in the upstairs bedroom in Vermont.

I then took Nina to lunch in a cafe in a building containing what used to be a very famous restaurant, dating back before the Revolution. The cafe was well-filled and obviously popular. Nina, who hasn't been able to afford a restaurant in several years and is very tired of cooking, thought the cafe extremely expensive and was shocked to see all the patrons, some quite young. "Where do they get the money?" she kept asking. "They live in a way we don't understand at all, Boris and I. I look at them and I think I have been left behind, like the dinosaurs. It is a very unpleasant feeling."

The food was so-so—a ham and cheese dish, a little salad of tomatoes and cucumbers, which we shared, bread, and a couple of Pepsis, rather flat. A meager repast. There were no napkins, although there were tablecloths and, most important, chairs. I sat on a low banquette and Nina on a chair. Between us was a round table with an immensely heavy metal base that made it impossible to push the table close enough to the banquette. Nevertheless, the atmosphere was restful, we enjoyed each other's company, and we got into conversation with a grey-bearded man at the next table who offered to sell us records from a stack of compact discs he had with him. I had been hoping to buy some cassettes of Russian folk music on balalaikas, but he had none and said they'd be hard to find, although American-style pop music was available everywhere. Nina said it would be easier to buy balalaika music in New York than Moscow.

Nina and I have become great friends. We talk about our husbands and our lives, and find things to laugh about. I've invited her and Boris to stay with us any time they're in the States. They'll be coming to Virginia next spring, so perhaps we'll see them.

Nina is one-quarter Russian. Her maternal grandfather was a moujik from Georgia, and her grandmother a Jew who converted to Christianity when she married. Nina grew up in the Moscow apartment that had been her grandparents' before the Revolution. The Russian grandfather was uneducated but intelligent. He was educated by his wife, so well that he eventually became a well-known professor of literature.

Nina's life has changed a great deal in the last three years. She married Boris, who is her boss at the Institute, after the death of the husband to whom she'd been married for thirty years. She said the two men were very different. Her first husband, a law professor, had a very high governmental position; he was the only Jew on some governing body (I've forgotten the name), and had other distinctions. A man with many friends, he was a more sociable creature than the austere, intellectual Boris who, according to Nina, never wants to go out or do anything of a purely social nature, and has colleagues but no friends. She, though, has women friends. She feels displaced, without a home. The apartment in the suburbs was Boris's and is furnished according to his taste. The apartment in town where she lived for many years and still spends time is now the home of her daughter, son-in-law, and granddaughter. Her own dacha is rented, and when the Ioffes go to the country they stay with Boris's brother, who is "peculiar," although he has a nice wife.

Boris, too, grew up in Moscow in a downtown flat that had belonged to his parents and grandparents. The location was convenient—livelier and more interesting, he said, than the suburb where he now lives—but it was a communal flat, with one kitchen and one bathroom shared by six families; that is, twenty people. Their present apartment is larger and is theirs alone.

Nina told me about Boris's tribulations at the Institute, a place he virtually created from nothing. He's now constantly harassed by money worries. The support just isn't there and he has to watch the steady chipping away of what he has built, a very unhappy situation for him.

Boris's life as a scientist—a fine scientist—and a Jew in Russia has been far from easy. When he was finishing his graduate studies he was offered a prestigious job in an institute where he would be the only Jew. However, just at that time he contracted dysentery and became so ill he had to be hospitalized. His recovery was slow, and the doctor said he would have to postpone his Ph. D.; yet he knew that if he lost a year he would never have another chance at the job he wanted. It was necessary to choose. Against medical advice he left the hospital after only a couple of weeks, managed to complete his studies, and took the position he had been offered. He has paid a heavy price though, for his health never fully recovered and he has been plagued by stomach disorders all his life. He is a thin, pale, gray, rather frail-looking man and a chronic worrier. Although he has been extremely kind to me, and Nina says he would probably describe himself as a mild, gentle person, she feels quite dominated by him. Nina appears to be the fiery, temperamental one, but Boris wields a remarkably effective veto, and she feels she can't have anything the way she wants it.

Saturday, August 22, 1992, Minsk, Yasha and Marina Shnir's apartment. I am the first American either Yasha or Marina has ever seen in Minsk. These are intellectuals, both of them physicists. Yasha once met an Englishman in Minsk, but an American? Never.

Of course I had no time or energy to write in my journal yesterday. I got up early in the Ioffes' apartment, organized my belongings for the trip to Minsk, and packed. I am carrying money in three places: a zippered money belt concealed under my clothes contains enough to cover the contingencies I'm fairly sure of before I go home, chiefly rent and a payment to Yasha for his services as a guide and interpreter; an additional wad of bills in a plastic bag in my trousers pocket, which I have secured from inside with a safety pin; and a small amount in the waist pouch worn outside my clothes, which is serving as my pocketbook during the trip. Boris warned me, "You must be careful every moment. Do not let anyone see that you are carrying of money. Try not to let people know you speak English.

I asked Boris's advice about how much to pay Yasha Shnir for his help, and an appropriate payment for my overnight stays in private apartments. Boris thought twenty dollars a night in American money would be acceptable for the latter. "As for Shnir—this is more delicate."

"I don't want to offend him."

"You must realize he is not a guide. He is not a student. He is a physicist."

"How old is he?"

"About thirty-five. He is quite a good physicist, actually, but his salary is only about twenty dollars a month. I am not sure you have to pay him anything."

"Of course I'm going to pay him. I have no other way to thank him. He's taking time off from work, he has a car, he's putting himself at my disposal for four days, he's already gone to a lot of trouble. And I don't even know him. How about twenty dollars a night for my two nights in his apartment, and something like fifty dollars a day, plus the gas and other expenses—"

"Too much, too much!" Boris was shocked. "For him this would be an enormous fortune! And the gas is nothing, it is cheap. Forget about the gas." He pondered. "If he ends up with a hundred and fifty dollars at the end of it, he will be very happy. You must realize these people in Belarus are on the edge of actual want. For those who have no access to hard currency, especially, the situation is quite dangerous."

The "situation"—this is the word people use to refer to the inflation, the social breakdown, and the overall social chaos.

I packed some gifts for the Shnirs in a plastic bag: a box of gold-wrapped chocolates, a box of chocolate pudding mix, a canned ham, a pound of coffee, a tube of hand cream, and other odds and ends.

As I was finishing my packing Boris knocked on my door. All smiles he informed me he'd managed to reach the taxi company, and a cab would be picking me up at half past one.

This should be plenty of time, as the plane for Minsk leaves at five-thirty. There will be time, after all, for me to return to the Old Arbat this morning. I liked some Palekh-like paintings I saw yesterday of Russian scenes, on slabs of wood about five by seven inches, and want to buy enough to present one to each of my cousins at the cousins' reunion in November as a symbol of our Russian roots, about which I hope to learn more when I am in Belarus.

I was nervous about going downtown again; not fearful of the trip this time, but worried that some contingency might prevent me from returning in time for the taxi. Clearly, it would be no easy matter to get another. Still, it seemed cowardly to waste my last morning in Moscow hiding out in Boris and Nina's apartment, so I decided to chance it.

Boris sat me down ceremoniously at the dining room table, I took out my small pocket notebook, and he gave me directions in his usual fantastically accurate and detailed style, drawing me diagrams of escalators and tunnels, and writing out the names of subway stops in Russian and in English. He then squired me to the subway stop, a different one than I'd taken before, pausing at each turn in the path, telling me to turn around, and impressing on me the landmarks so I could make my way back alone. I told him that with his directions to guide me I could go to the moon. It was cloudy and I brought my umbrella. All my days in Moscow have been grey and rainy.

Boris gave me strict instructions to enter the metro for the return trip no later than twelve noon, and feeling like Cinderella I parted from him.

It was 10:15 when I reached the Old Arbat. The Palekh sellers were just setting up their stalls. Only a few were open for business, which was just as well—the choice was less bewildering. I purchased seven of the Palekh paintings for twenty-five dollars, and other gifts as well, and was back in the subway by eleven. When I reached the Ioffes' flat at twelve, Boris was doing the laundry. Nina had told me, "Of course the laundry is a man's job because it requires strength."

Lev Okun called, wanting to speak to me; he has just returned to Moscow, but I won't see him until next week, when he is coming to Stockholm for a meeting. He congratulated me on my wedding anniversary, which he'd heard, god knows how, that Joe and I had just celebrated. He and his wife have been married about as long as we have. I told him, "We're veterans of a long campaign."

III. The Flight to Minsk

Boris knocked on my door. "Now I must give you your final instructions."

Again we sat down at the dining room table, again I took out my pocket notebook. With a serious look he informed me, "You must pay the driver seven hundred rubles, not more. I have calculated the number of miles to the airport, and the rate per mile. I have added the sixty ruble charge for coming to the house, and a little more to cover various possibilities. You must positively not pay more. But—" He raised a cautionary forefinger. "You must not speak. If the driver hears you speak English, right away it will be twenty dollars. The trouble is, once the taxi leaves, the driver will ask you how you want to go to the airport. Of course you cannot answer. I think it is best if you pretend to be mute."

I looked at him. "Boris, you've got to be kidding."

"Well—perhaps I can tell him that you do not know the way. If he doesn't know how to get to the airport, I will tell him before you leave."

I agreed to this proposal. Then he described all the things that could and probably would go wrong at the airport. There might be no list of flights posted. If there was, it would be necessary to find out if the flights were on time or delayed; if delayed, I would be unable to understand the announcements made over the loudspeaker, and they would be posted on the list, if there was one, only after a considerable delay, if at all. There might be shortages of petrol. If I checked my bag, the contents would quite possibly be stolen; no matter how heavy it was (loaded with canned hams and sardines, it was very heavy) I should try to carry it on board. If this was impossible, all I could do was hope for the best. He didn't think the bag itself would vanish, only the contents. Did I have a lock?

"No."

He sighed. The flight might be delayed many hours, or even until the next day; of course if that happened I was to call him and return to the flat.

I said my farewells to Boris, thanked him, and told him he must stay with us whenever he is in America. I'd already said goodbye to Nina that morning before she went to work, with warm hugs and a few tears on both sides at the thought that it might be a very long time before we met again, if ever.

The taxi took off. I cowered in a corner as inconspicuously as possible, saying not a word, recalling Boris's warnings about the dangers associated with taxis and hoping I wasn't about to be kidnapped. I wasn't wearing any makeup—I figured it was desirable to look depressed, and blend into the crowd.

I had a fine view of Moscow from the taxi, and recognized quite a few landmarks I'd been too disoriented, when I'd first come from the airport, to appreciate properly. We passed a number of churches and monasteries, the only buildings of any architectural merit. So far I haven't been able to whip up any enthusiasm for visiting them because their link with the rabid anti-Semitism of the country makes them repellent to me.

The ride was very long. I began to recognize the terrain near the airport and told myself that if I was being kidnapped, there was no particular reason for the driver to take me to the airport to do it, a reassuring thought.

In fact, we drew up before the domestic terminal without incident. Although I hadn't said a word, when the driver turned around he addressed me in English. I handed him the seven hundred rubles I'd prepared. He took it with a smile and asked for no more money.

I went inside.

The domestic terminal, unlike the international one, was shabby, dirty, and very crowded. Despite Boris's dire prognostications, a notice board was prominently displayed, listing flights in Russian and in English. The flight to Minsk was expected to leave on time. I was three hours early—plenty of time to consume a plate of meat and rice in the cafe, and inspect the tacky kiosks with their displays of western-style T-shirts and jeans and a polyester dress or two, and the folding table where a young man was selling Marlboro cigarettes. These are immensely popular in Russia, and I'd brought three packs with me but haven't needed them yet.

The woman in the information booth spoke no English and referred me to Intourist, poking the air vaguely with her finger to indicate direction. I decided to avoid Intourist. Travelling on my own feels illicit in Russia, and I have fears of being captured and clapped into a guided tour group. I sat down and drank some of the boiled water I've been carry-ing in a plastic bottle, which I refilled from Nina's kettle this morning. I'm being very care-ful, in hopes of avoiding travelers' diarrhea; so far, so good.

Three quarters of an hour before my flight was to leave I went investigating and found a cluster of people at a ticket counter. There was no sign, so I wrote my flight number, the word "MINSK" in Cyrillic, and a large question mark on a piece of paper and showed it to a Russian woman. She gazed at me in astonishment, studied the paper, comprehension dawned and she nodded. I said, "Minsk?"

She said, "Minsk."

I waited a while, but nothing seemed to be happening. I tapped the woman on the shoulder and pointed to my suitcase. She shook her ticket at me so I showed her mine. By this time the people around me were aware I wasn't Russian and were watching me with interest, and when I showed my ticket an amazed murmur went around the crowd because it was different from theirs. One man who looked more intelligent than the oth-ers snatched it, examined it, and explained something to the others in which I caught a word that seemed to mean "foreign." The crowd then thrust me forward until I reached the counter. I plopped my suitcase on the weighing platform and waved my ticket in the face of the agent. She took it and exclaimed, "Intourist! Intourist!" A man behind the counter grabbed my bag and made off with it, the agent gestured urgently for me to step up on the platform. Was I to be publicly weighed? No, fortunately. The agent seized my hand and pulled me behind the counter, shoving me toward the man who was disap-pearing with my bag. I scurried after him to the far end of the terminal where Intourist awaited in the person of a blond woman who spoke English and sized up the situation at once. Efficiently labelling my bag and issuing me a boarding pass, she told me to go up the steps and through the security check.

I followed her instructions, but as I passed through the security gate a guard barked something at me in Russian.

"Sorry," I said. "I'm afraid I only speak English."

Stony-faced, he pointed at my waist pouch, which was rolling off the X-ray conveyer belt, and indicated I was to open it. When I did, he pointed at the cylindrical plastic inhaler, which I carry in case of an asthma attack and which no one has ever questioned before. I tapped my chest and imitated a coughing fit, at which after a moment he nodded and waved me through.

Eventually I found myself boarding a plane which was probably going to Minsk. I seemed to have no seat reservation, and since no one spoke English, including the stewardess, I simply sat down up front where four seats faced each other, two and two, with a table in between. The seatbelt in the aisle seat was too short to go around my ample waist—long a nightmare of mine, but the first time this had actually happened—so I moved to the window seat where the belt was longer, despite the voluble protests of a large, grey-bearded man with a deep voice and an air of authority who sat in the window seat opposite, and with whose knees, it was clear, mine were going to have to interact in an intimate manner. He tried to get me to remain where I was, and I gave a demonstration of the nature of the belt problem. He laughed in a friendly fashion and then took charge of my transfer to the window seat, the stowing of my carry-on bag, the fastening of my seatbelt, and the arrangement of my knees. I said, "Minsk?"

He nodded. "Minsk."

Passengers loaded with enormous bundles and leading dogs on leashes flowed down the aisle. Two men appeared and demanded my seat; they had reservations. The grey-haired man defended my squatters' rights vigorously. The stewardess appeared, and the three appealed to her. The grey-haired man did most of the talking, but the other two kept waving their reservations and eventually I was transferred across the aisle to a seat where a child had been sitting, after the child had climbed on her mother's lap. The space beneath my seat was occupied by one of the mother's bags, but the grey-haired man took charge of my carry-on bag, placing it on the table before him, where it remained for the rest of the flight. The stewardess made no protest, and I could only hope the flight would be smooth; since the bag weighed about twenty pounds, it would make a lethal projectile.

The motors began to turn. Despite Boris's fears, we were leaving right on time. I arranged my knees and leaned my head back as we taxied down the runway and the tensions of the day drained away. I was off to Belarus, land of my forebears, where my great-grandfather had been murdered and from which my grandfather had fled.

IV. Minsk

The plane banked and began its descent. From the air I gazed down on a flat agricultural country where swathes of dark forest clasped broad patches of fields under cultivation, some green and others yellow. A river snaked in lazy coils from north to south, the Dnieper of my grandfather's tales. Sunlight blazed in an intensely blue sky. It seemed a smiling land after the gray of Moscow, not the grim, haunted, country of my imagination but a realm of golden brightness. A gossamer haze quivered in the air like a barely visible veil; from the earth rose columns of mist. From lakes, perhaps? I saw no lakes. Then I realized the columns were smoke from the fires I'd read about. Drought had seared this land all summer, and now the fields were burning.

My Guide: Yasha Shnir

At the gate a handsome young man stood like a sentry at attention, arms at his sides, and a piece of cardboard with my name on it dangling from his hand. This was Yasha Shnir, who was to be my guide and interpreter. As I approached he surveyed me with calm attention. He had dark brown hair and a dark mustache, a short, straight nose, full cheeks, and alert, rather small dark eyes with an upward tilt at the corners that gave his face a Mongolian cast. It was a face that could have been Jewish, as I knew he was, or Georgian, Italian, or Spanish. He seemed very young to me; whatever his experience of life had been, so far it had left his face unmarked by any emotion except watchfulness.

We greeted each other, and he said he had feared he'd missed me, as another plane from Moscow had landed only an hour earlier. He apologized for his English, which was halting but fairly good, and as we walked through the small terminal he apologized again, this time for his car, which he explained was a twenty-year-old Lada.

I said, "Does it run?"

"It runs, yes. Last year I had to repair the engine, but now it runs."

He stowed my suitcase in the back seat, which had been re-covered with a flowered fabric, rejecting my suggestion that we put it in the trunk. "No, no, I am sorry but the trunk is very dirty." As he bowed me into the front seat he said, "I have heard of your husband, of course."

The car seemed adequate, and I was more than ready, after the Moscow subway, to be chauffeured down a smooth, four-lane highway between sunny fields which he said belonged to a local kolkhoz, or collective farm. I saw no one working in the fields—I soon learned this wasn't unusual—but lines of cut hay wavered off toward the horizon, and some had already been piled into stacks the size and shape of houses. A warm wind ruffled my hair and I said, "The heat feels good. It rained the whole time I was in Moscow."

He replied, "I am tired of hot weather."

The air had an acrid undercurrent that made me wonder how many radioactive particles I was inhaling as we sped toward Minsk, but we saw no fires. We spoke of Isaac Asimov, who had been a brother of Yasha's grandfather. The Russian branch of the family, he said, had never tried to get in touch with their famous relative, who had gone to America in his youth; it might have been dangerous for them if the connection had become known. When I described a brief conversation I'd once had with Asimov at a conference he was fascinated, for "unfortunately"—it was a word I was to hear him use often—he, himself, had never met Asimov, and in fact had only learned he was his uncle four years earlier.

He informed me he'd made two brief, professional trips outside Russia, and spoke of Italy, where he'd spent two weeks at a physics institute, with an appreciation bordering on ecstasy.

I asked if he planned to come to the United States, and he shook his head. "I cannot." His hands tightened on the wheel as he stared at the road ahead. "I have an invita-

Burning Fields

tion to visit a laboratory in Chicago for three weeks, and also one in Boulder, Colorado, but the plane is too expensive. I asked my institute would they pay for the ticket, and they refused. You understand, I and another colleague, a friend you will meet tomorrow, are the only ones who have been outside Russia. The others think, 'Why do they get these invitations and not us?'" I recalled Boris Ioffe's saying that Yasha was a good physicist; Boris did not give praise lightly. "It would cost me five hundred dollars to go, and I earn twenty dollars a month. So you see it is impossible."

Very well, I thought. He has told me what he wants, perhaps what he hopes for from me. I understand the situation.

We rocketed down the road in silence. The car was noisy but comfortable enough, and my companion a fast and accurate driver. He remarked, "My grandfather was born in 1884, exactly the same year as yours. Mine stayed in Belarus, of course. He had a little shop. He managed to survive the war, but under Stalin he was imprisoned in a gulag because he was a Jew. Maybe if he had gone to America, now I—" He shrugged. "Tell me, why have you come to Belarus? What is it you want to do here?"

It was the same question Boris had asked me; again I felt inadequate to answer it. "I don't know," I said slowly. "I never really decided to come, I didn't believe I would do it, it just—happened. I don't have specific things I want to do each day. Maybe you can make suggestions. I've thought about writing a novel based on my grandfather's life, and I wanted to see what the country he came from looked like. But maybe I'll never write it—I don't know if I can, actually. The books I've written before have been mysteries."

He smiled. "My wife likes detective stories."

"It's possible the book might turn out to be a mystery. There's a story in the family that my great-grandfather was murdered in an apple orchard. Apparently there was a custom around the turn of the century for people to rent an orchard, take care of it for a season, and then have the right to sell the fruit. Have you ever heard of that?"

"No, never."

"Well, perhaps the story isn't true. But supposedly my great-grandfather was guarding the orchard one night, and someone killed him with a club and stole the fruit."

"Do you know who?"

"No, and I never will. I'll have to make it up."

"And you can do that."

"Of course." After a moment I added, "But also I just want to see where my family came from. Even if I never write a word about it."

"Are you hoping to find relatives?"

"No. In fact I'm sure I won't. There were two elderly women who survived the war— my grandfather used to get letters from them, and my grandmother sent them packages of clothes. But this was forty years ago; by now they must be dead."

Ahead of us, small houses climbed a slope. They were packed closely together, each in its patch of garden. I asked, "Is that a village?"

"No, those are dachas belonging to people from Minsk. They use them on the weekend. But as for villages—unfortunately, many of them have disappeared, Jewish villages especially. The Nazis killed the people and burned the houses. Some villages have been rebuilt, others not. I am afraid you may be disappointed."

I shook my head. "I'm not really expecting anything in particular. I'm not here to look for a relative, or a house, or a grave. I know I may go to Streshin and find absolutely nothing. If that happens, so be it. Don't worry that I'll be disappointed. Nothing is something, too."

We looked at each other. He nodded as if he understood. I wondered if what I'd said was true, or only the way I was trying to feel. I'd told myself to abandon all expectations, all preconceptions, in order to experience fully whatever adventures the journey would bring.

Yet surely I hoped to find something....

Massive new apartment houses sprang up on the horizon as we neared the outskirts of Minsk. "They are always building," said Yasha. "Minsk was totally destroyed during the war. Everything you will see was built after 1950."

Everything? How could that be true? A city couldn't be totally destroyed. He had to be exaggerating, surely something remained of the past.

The apartment houses gathered us in. Twelve-story monoliths of reinforced concrete, they sprawled with a crushing weight on the bare, parched earth, their cliff-like sides sprouting miniscule balconies. Did people sit outside, I wondered, inhaling the exhaust fumes that fouled the air, and the smoke, and the radioactive particles that might or might not be there? On all but the newest buildings, the cement was cracked and crumbling and stained with rust; big chunks had fallen off. I said, "How many people live in Minsk?"

"The population is two million. Minsk is the largest city in Belarus." He added doubtfully, "Tomorrow if you like I can show you around, but there is not much to see. It is an industrial city. Perhaps the museum—" We were entering the heart of the city. A few public buildings appeared, and then a downtown area where traces of bourgeois decoration—a few stone swags and garlands—had been affixed to the facades.

Yasha informed me expressionlessly that the broader avenues had been laid out, under Stalin, by demolishing cemeteries and the few remaining pre-revolutionary build-

Minsk: Downtown

ings that had managed to survive the war. We passed an imposing structure that was the military headquarters, and then a military college. "My father was a colonel in the army," said Yasha. "He was stationed in Minsk, so I grew up here. But my grandfather came from a village, like yours."

Downtown there were many trees, their shade dappling the sidewalks; already in mid-August the leaves were yellowing, and some had fallen on the tufts of trodden straw that were all that remained of the lawns. Here and there flower beds had fallen victim to the drought. Yet the people we passed looked less depressed than those in Moscow, and the city seemed cleaner, in somewhat better repair, and not unpleasant, despite the polluted air.

Yasha said, "The present population of Minsk is exactly what it was before the war. But at that time sixty percent of the people were Jews, and now there are only twenty-five thousand of us."

We drove in silence for a while. Then he turned into a side street. A strip of parkway bordered the road, where a tree-shaded promenade followed the shining curve of the Dnieper. "This is pretty," I said.

"I walk here almost every day with my daughter." "How old is she?" I had known he had a child, and wondered what she would be doing while her father escorted a strange American woman through Belarus.

"She is two and a half years."

"I have four children, all grown up."

"Four!"

He steered the Lada into a driveway, as I thought about the million Jews who had died. Suddenly the mere existence of Yasha, so young and full of life, with a little daughter, seemed to me a miracle.

I said, "I don't want you to worry about feeding me while I'm here. I've brought my own food, enough for a week."

"Well—tonight we won't think about it. Marina has made dinner." He pulled the Lada into a small parking area beside the door of an apartment house that looked like all the others. Then he switched off the motor and turned to face me, smiling. "Dorothy, we are here."

Marina met us at the door of the apartment. Coming up in the elevator, Yasha had told me with some pride that she was a theoretical physicist who would be getting her

Ph.D. in a few weeks. I'd wondered what she would look like, and found her to be very pretty, tall and slender with dark, flowing hair and a shy manner. When I asked if she spoke English she giggled rather hysterically, blushed, and shook her head indicating that she did not. In fact this turned out to be untrue. She'd simply never had an occasion to speak it before.

She was delighted with the canned ham and the other small gifts I'd brought, and especially with a box of chocolate pudding mix over which she exclaimed joyfully, "Oh, I can make this for Olga!"

On the coffee table in the living room, we ate the dinner she'd prepared. Marina and I sat on the sofa, and Yasha pulled up a chair. I couldn't help speculating about how much it had cost her in time, not to mention money that could ill be spared, to procure the large, tender, juicy slices of veal she now served us, which she had breaded and sautéed in the Viennese manner. With it she offered us a dish of minced, fried potatoes and a salad of fresh cucumbers, tomatoes, and parsley. The vegetables had come, she confided proudly, "from the dacha." The food was delicious and I ate with pleasure, repressing stray thoughts about radiation levels, as I was to do throughout my stay in Belarus. It was just as well I'd spent a lifetime avoiding chest and dental X-rays, I decided; this week

Marina, Dorothy and Yasha

I would make up for it. I wondered how my hosts managed to live and raise a child under the lingering threat from Chernobyl; but it seemed too soon to bring the subject up.

Olga, they said, was spending the summer at the dacha with her grandparents. I asked to see her picture, and Marina obliged by bringing out a large stack. As Yasha protested, "Too many pictures!" we went through them, and I assured him, truthfully, that I was enjoying it. Showing the pictures of her small blonde daughter relaxed Marina, who began to speak English more freely and to smile, revealing her dimples and a couple of gold-capped teeth at the sides of her mouth. After a while she remarked, "I am surprised how much people from different places are alike."

I said, "You mean me?" She nodded. "What did you imagine I'd be like?"

"I didn't know. I never saw an American before."

"No?"

"I never heard of an American in Minsk."

"Really?" I turned to Yasha. "What about you?"

"You are the first American I have ever seen in Minsk. Once I met an Englishman, but an American, never."

I was astonished. Surely these two young professionals must be fairly sophisticated people, for Minsk. I, their first American? In that case, I

Left, Olga and, right, Marina

should try to be more entertaining—it would be bad if their first American turned out to be a dud.

I began to explain what had led up to my trip to Russia.

"For some reason the whole thing seemed to start after my mother died three years ago," I said. "I found myself thinking all the time about my childhood, and especially about my grandparents, who had died twenty years before. I had been very close to them, and used to spend summers at their place in the country, just as your Olga is doing with her grandparents now.

"Some people loved my grandparents, including myself, but many others hated them. They were complicated people. My grandfather had started out as a carpenter with three rubles in his pocket when he came to America, but eventually he became a builder, and quite wealthy. He brought many of his relatives over from Streshin, which some of them appreciated; others thought he should have done more for them. Maybe it was his money that started all the trouble, and maybe it was the way my grandparents used it, pitting their children against each other, and giving them money instead of love. Anyway, after a while a feud developed."

"A normal thing in families," commented Yasha.

"True, but this was extreme. Two of their four children ended up not speaking to the other two for many years, and this carried over to their children—my generation—and to the grandchildren and so on. When my grandparents died and it was learned they'd disinherited two of their children, matters became still worse.

"Personally, I'd never quarreled with any of my relatives, but I inherited the feud just like everyone else. My mother would have considered it very disloyal if I'd had anything to do with the "other" side.

"I was an only child, yet while I was growing up I'd had this enormous family of aunts, uncles, cousins, and distant relations. All of them—at least the older generation—had come to America from Streshin. They formed a society called "the Streshiners" that used to meet in my grandparents' basement three or four times a year.

"But somehow by the time I'd grown up, I hardly seemed to have any family at all. I'd lived on the same street as my seven first cousins and we'd played together as children, yet I hadn't spoken to any of them in years; we were scattered all over the United States and didn't bother to keep in touch.

"For many years I didn't particularly care. My husband and I were living our own lives and raising our children. We were intellectuals, we travelled, we had friends—I felt I had nothing in common with all those people I'd known as a child, who just happened to be related to me by blood.

"And then, as I've said, something changed, something in me. I began dragging old letters and papers down from the attic and reading through them. I went through boxes of family photographs, some of them taken in Russia and dating back ninety years. It became an obsession. I devoured books about the history of the Jews in Russia, and Jewish immigrant life in America, subjects I'd never had the slightest interest in before. If anything, I'd made a point of ignoring the fact that I was Jewish, as if it had nothing to do with me. I didn't want to feel all that pain. I didn't want to think about anti-Semitism, or face the fact that it still exists and could conceivably affect me or my children.

"Now, though, I wanted to know more and more. I could make up theories of why this happened, but the truth is, I really don't know. Probably a book was germinating—but why this particular book, and why just then? My mother's death seemed to have freed me to acknowledge the emptiness I felt at the loss of my family, a family she'd rejected and I'd neglected. I needed to explore the part of me that was Jewish, which she, a child of immigrants who'd tried desperately to assimilate, had spent a lifetime repudiating.

"I'd reached a certain age, my children were grown, and it was time for me to look back at my life and understand it in a new way—not just as the life of an individual, but as a link in a chain.

"One day I took out my mother's address book, which I'd put away after her death, and started going through it. All the telephone numbers were there, of relatives she hadn't spoken to in decades. I began to call people. Naturally they were very surprised to hear from me, but most of them were receptive. A few very elderly relatives were still living in Florida, and I decided to pay them a visit. I wanted them to tell me what they remembered about the family, before it was too late. And although it felt very strange, I did fly down to Florida and spend a week there, driving down the coast, visiting relatives, and taping our conversations—with their permission, of course. The word of my activities was spreading, and everybody wondered what I was up to. Most of them seemed to assume I was some sort of judge, come to decide who'd been right and who'd been wrong about all those old arguments; who'd been "good" and who'd been "bad." Still, they welcomed me. I received a letter from a third cousin with an interest in Jewish history; she offered her help. Another cousin, who lived in Florida, invited me to stay with her for a few days, although she was on the "other" side.

"It turned out to be a wonderful week, and at the end of it, while I was staying at my cousin Lois's house, we visited the grave of my grandparents, whom I had loved and she had hated, and afterwards she suggested we try to hold a reunion of the seven surviving first cousins a few months later at her house in Miami, which was very big and—yes, Yasha and Marina—had palm trees and a swimming pool in the back yard, just like in the movies.

"This reunion did take place, although one of the seven cousins refused to come, and another didn't even reply to the invitation. The five of us spent an entire weekend together, talking about our childhoods and our lives as adults, and always returning to the subject of our grandparents, of whom we have such vivid and differing memories, and about whose motives we never seem to get tired of speculating.

"Since then we've kept in touch by telephone and letter, visited each other's homes, and attended the wedding of Lois's son. A second reunion is supposed to take place in three months, this time in New York. The cousin who refused to come last year is planning to attend, and the rest of us are eager to see him and hear his story. Of course I intend to give my cousins a full report on my visit to Russia; in fact, in a way I feel I'm really representing the whole family."

"A very interesting story," said Yasha.

"But weren't you afraid to come to Belarus, all by yourself?" asked Marina.

"Of course I was! What do you think? I was petrified! I don't know the language or even the alphabet, the country is in chaos, there's inflation, no food, people told me I'd get mugged, everything's radioactive—"

"You must be a very brave woman."

"Well—I don't know about brave. We have a saying, 'fools rush in where angels fear to tread.'"

They looked at me blankly.

"Fools"—I twirled my finger at my temple and put on a stupid expression—"rush in"—I got up and dashed across the living room—"where angels"—flapping my arms seraphically—"fear to tread." My hands clasped in prayer, I took a few cautious, mincing steps.

"I think I will come with you tomorrow," said Marina.

After they left I explored the apartment. This didn't take long, for it consisted of one big room, a small kitchen, and a bathroom. A narrow balcony, glassed in by Yasha to cut down on the noise from the street below, gave them some storage space and room for Marina's potted plants.

The couch I was to sleep on was the one Yasha and Marina usually shared, though tonight they were sleeping at her parents' apartment. A few feet away against the opposite wall stood Olga's crib, with a flaxen-haired doll tucked cozily under a blanket, its head on a pillow. There were a couple of bookcases, a desk, the coffee table on which we'd eaten dinner, a TV set, a stereo and a collection of records, a large wardrobe, and two chairs. The furniture was faded and undistinguished, the flowered wallpaper looked as if left over from a previous tenant, and a flimsy curtain covered the windows. A calendar over the desk provided an incongruous note, with its picture of a wholesomely seductive blonde in pantyhose coyly crossing her hands over her breasts. The room was somehow pleasant and not at all depressing; I felt at home there.

I took a shower, rinsed out a couple of sweaty T-shirts, and helped myself to a glass of creamy milk and a slice of the blueberry cake Marina had baked for dessert. Ignoring my protests, Yasha had opened the couch ("Unfortunately, it is broken") before he'd left, and as soon as I lay down on it I dropped into a heavy sleep.

Promptly at eleven the next morning, Yasha and Marina reappeared. With them was Yasha's colleague, Valery, who had spent more time abroad than Yasha and whose English was somewhat more fluent. He had a delicate build and a bony, clever, androgynous face, and was the father of a little boy Olga's age, whose photograph I'd seen the night before. He didn't look Jewish, but when I later asked Yasha, he told me he was "half and half." Knowing whether people were or weren't Jewish had an importance for me in Russia that it had never had at home; the Russian Jews had had certain experiences, chiefly those deriving from anti-Semitism, and therefore shared certain assumptions. Jews could be trusted—maybe not all, but most of the ones I would meet.

I succumbed immediately to Valery's sweetness and humor. In contrast to Yasha he was expressive, while Yasha seemed more intense and self-contained. He told me he, too, had never seen an American in Minsk.

We got into the Lada with Yasha at the wheel and me in the front seat beside him, while Marina and Valery sat in back. Our plan was to spend the day in and around Minsk. The next morning, Yasha and I would head south toward Streshin, which none of them had heard of before my arrival. They seemed somewhat doubtful of its existence, although it was marked in tiny letters on the map of Western Russia I'd brought with me. Yasha was very surprised when I produced this map, as he himself does not possess a road map of the area; all three young people studied it with as much interest as if they'd never seen one before. Yasha mentioned that when he and Marina had gone hiking in the Urals, they'd had to do so without a map.

Valery, however, had brought along a good map of Minsk and environs, and after consulting it we set out for Khatyn, a memorial of World War II I wanted to see, after reading about it in my guidebook. Written by two adventurous young men and subtitled "A Survival Guide to the USSR," this book had been published only the year before, and was already out of date due to the rapid changes that were taking place. Still, I'd found it useful, although the section on Belarus was rather brief. The others, curious to know how their country was perceived by the outside world, were as interested in the guidebook as they'd been in the map. "Living in Belorussia," said Marina, "I sometimes feel very—I don't know the word."

"Isolated?"

"Yes. Isolated. Exactly. That is a good word."

I asked her if she was planning to work as a physicist once she got her degree."

"Not now. I must take care of Olga."

Yasha said, "She is what you call a housewife."

"And when Olga starts school?"

"Then, yes, I would like very much. But—"She bit her lip, her brow wrinkling unhappily. "I don't think I will find a job. Not as a physicist. It is very difficult."

Yasha said, "When I got my Ph. D. I could not get a physics appointment. Maybe it was because of my nationality, I don't know." 'Nationality,' I was aware by now, meant Jewishness. "I like my nationality, I would not wish to change it. But—"He shrugged. "I had to work for six years as a schoolteacher. Then I had an opportunity for a position at my institute, and of course I took it. There are hardly any Jews there."

What a shame, I thought. What a loss. I've heard physicists say, many times, that physics is a "young man's game." There are those, like my husband, who continue to be productive when they're older, but it remains true that most of the greatest discoveries have required the passionate energies of youth.

We headed north, passing a block-long building that is the headquarters of the KGB. I said, "What are the KGB agents doing, now that the Cold War is over?"

The others looked at each other. Finally Valery said, "That is a very good question. Maybe they are still doing the same thing. We do not know. But none of them are out of a job."

The day was overcast, and as we passed the outskirts of Minsk and headed north toward Khatyn, the air thickened and I began to smell smoke. Soon we were in the country. Hayfields alternated with forests. We passed some cows, not many, and I asked who they belonged to.

"Probably the Kolkhoz," said Valery. "Especially if they are thin cows."

"Are there any family farms, private farms?"

"Now, yes. The laws are changing, they are being discussed. It is a big controversy. There are very few private farmers; it is hard for them to buy land. The kolkhozes will not sell to them, except land that is very poor. They see them as competitors. Now these private farmers are banding together to fight for their rights. We hear about it on the television."

The two-lane road we were following was narrow, though in good repair. Yasha drove expertly and fast, swerving out to pass the trucks and slower-moving cars as Marina bleated softly but persistently in Russian. I said, "Marina is giving you instructions?"

"Instructions, yes," said Yasha with a husbandly exasperation that transcended national boundaries. "Instructions, unfortunately."

I confessed that I, too, gave instructions when my husband was driving, and taught them the term, "back-seat driver." This they seemed to find irresistibly amusing; at least, they kept returning to it all day.

The pall of smoke over the road was becoming thicker. My throat felt sore. I began to worry about my asthma, and was glad I'd brought along the inhaler that had so alarmed the security man at the Moscow airport.

We were driving straight toward the fires, and the road soon entered a patch of woodland from which heavy smoke was rising. There was no sign of flames, perhaps because it had rained during the night. Nobody spoke. Exchanging uneasy glances we kept on going.

Soon the smoke lessened. A ray or two of sunlight appeared, and the air became easier to breathe. We kept passing hot spots like this one during the 35-mile drive to Khatyn, smoldering unattended alongside the road. No one was making any effort to put them out. The smoke thickened and thinned, thickened and thinned.

When we were almost there, Yasha remarked that he knew of a rather good restaurant not far from Khatyn; at least, it had been good before "the situation" had become so severe. We decided to visit the memorial first, and then head for the restaurant. To cheer ourselves up, I thought without saying it. The memorial was sure to be a somber place, yet it seemed a fitting start for a journey through Belarus.

The village of Khatyn was a center of partisan activity during the Nazi occupation of Belarus. After a partisan attack in which several German soldiers were killed, the Nazis herded all 150 inhabitants of the town—men, women, and children— into the largest building and set it on fire, burning them alive. Anyone who attempted to escape was shot. Afterwards, all the houses in the village were totally destroyed. One man somehow managed to survive, and Valery told me he had actually met him, when he was a very old man.

The monument extended over several acres, the site of the former village of Khatyn, which for many years nestled in this cup-shaped vale rimmed by trees. Where each house once stood, a concrete post has been erected, bearing a plaque with the names and ages of the inhabitants, some only a few weeks old, and topped by a bell which tolled at irregular intervals. As we wandered the rough stone paths, which made for difficult walking, a bell would occasionally sound, now here, now there, like a voice calling from one of the vanished houses. Now and then a breeze swept over us bringing an acrid whiff of smoke, as if the fire that had consumed Khatyn was still smoldering.

Valery walked beside me, translating the inscriptions into English and whispering that 2,230,000 Belarusians had lost their lives during the war.

Straying off on my own, I came to a symbolic graveyard commemorating the 200 villages that had been obliterated, like Khatyn, during the Nazi occupation. Each had its house-size square of blackened cinders, its box containing soil from the spot where the village once stood, its pedestal the color of spilled blood, and its name carved on a low wall;

Left: Khatyn: Graveyard of the villages. Right: Monument at Khatyn.

these were lined up in rows that stretched away for a considerable distance.

I wondered if Streshin was among them. It was possible; why should one particular village have been spared? I thought of asking Valery if he saw the name of Streshin anywhere, but I didn't. If Streshin no longer existed I didn't want to be told about it, at least not yet and not here.

First I needed to go there.

We turned the car and headed back toward Minsk, and before long came to the restaurant Yasha had mentioned. It was a fairly large, not unattractive fieldstone building in the style of a rustic inn, the name of which meant "Green Pinewoods."

We went inside, where a few people were sitting at tables. Behind a glass counter were displayed a few dried-out pieces of fish, something that might have been chicken congealed in a gelatinous sauce, half a dozen slices of rye bread with salami on top, and a bowl of hard-boiled eggs. Further down the counter sat three or four shiny buns on a plate, and a slab of jelly roll. The buns didn't look bad.

No one was behind the counter, but two women in white aprons sat drinking tea at a table. Yasha and Valery approached them with determination, while Marina and I hung back; this was no job for women.

After several minutes of negotiation, the men returned with a crestfallen look. The women had said, they explained apologetically, that, in all honesty, they couldn't recommend we eat here because the food was very bad.

We stared at each other. By now we were hungry.

Yasha looked embarrassed, for it was he who had brought us here. Pessimistically he suggested, "Perhaps coffee?"

"Yes, coffee," I cried with false cheeriness, feeling that I ought to set an example of looking on the bright side, since I was the eldest as well as the guest. "And I'd simply love a bun. And perhaps a hardboiled egg."

Emboldened, the others, too, ordered coffee, with slices of jelly roll. I was refused a bun, as it was "from yesterday," but accepted a piece of the jelly roll. Yasha daringly ordered a salami sandwich. We took our food to a table, set it down, and studied it.

Finally, I cracked the egg on the tabletop. The noise seemed very loud. People were staring at us; they'd noticed I spoke English. "Eggs are safe," I remarked in a low, conversational tone. "Usually."

"Yes, I should have asked for one," agreed Yasha, as he pushed the salt in my direction, knocked it over, and blushed.

After a while Valery whispered, "How is the salami sandwich?"

Yasha said, "Not bad. All right."

Khatyn: Where they died.

"Then I think I will get one, too."

I said, "Is he your taster? Like in the court of the Chinese emperors? If he dies, you don't eat one?"

Valery grinned. "Sometimes he is the taster, sometimes I."

Yasha said grimly, "You see I am not dead. Yet."

When we got back to the car I said, "Okay. We have to have a serious conversation." They looked at me, alarmed. "It's about paying. I meant to take you all to lunch, but I couldn't figure out the damned rubles."

"But you are our guest," Yasha protested.

"I know, I know, and you're being absolutely wonderful and giving up all your time to entertain me, which I appreciate more than I can say. But I don't want you to spend any money. I mean it."

He said again, "You are our guest."

"I know, Yasha, I know. But the situation isn't normal. There's a terrible inflation. And I'm an American—you know it's different for me. Really, I insist. At least let me pay for my share of the lunch."

"Dorothy, forget about lunch," said Valery. "Truly, it was cheap, we can afford to pay. If you wish to take us out to dinner, I think that will be very nice."

I was relieved to find a pragmatist in the crowd. "Great! I'd love to take you all to dinner. Let's go to a good restaurant." After all, how much could it cost? I waited. No one raised any objection. "The best restaurant in Minsk! It's settled!" They nodded apprehensively. "And thank you for lunch!"

Valery had suggested we stop at the museum of Belarusian folk art outside Minsk; I had agreed, without enthusiasm. There seemed no reason to object though, for "sights" around Minsk were few. Parking the car at the foot of a hill, we climbed through woods to the summit and found the museum, housed in a lovely old church. "Unfortunately," as Yasha would have said, it was grotesquely framed by the girders of a gigantic ski jump, which some benighted commissar had decreed should be erected on this exact spot.

From the top of the hill we looked down on a sort of sports area containing a large rifle range, the targets lined up against one wall. Valery said that several international rifle competitions had been held here. Some years ago one of them (no doubt the last) had been in progress for three days when it was abruptly cancelled and moved to Norway, for reasons unspecified.

The museum proved to contain a number of turn-of-the-century peasant costumes that had been worn in the area around Gomel, not far from Streshin. These were the first objects I'd seen in Belarus that came from my grandfather's time and place, and I was beginning to fear they might prove to be the only ones. I'd never realized the extent to which the Nazis and then the Stalinists had devastated this country, and how little was left of its past. As I photographed the costumes sealed away in their cases, the disheartening thought occurred to me

Belarusian Folk Museum. Below: Traditional dress.

that the only relics I might ever find would be those in museums. America had museums aplenty, and there were even several devoted to Jewish history, which certainly wouldn't be the case here. I could always go to them; some I'd visited already.

I didn't really know why I'd come to Russia. It had never felt like a "decision," more like the inevitable outcome of a chain of events so long drawn out that, for all I knew, it had begun before my birth. I was simply here. I seemed to be looking for something. Whatever it was, I felt absolutely sure I wouldn't find it in a museum.

We came to a small village some distance from the road, and I asked if we could stop there. So far, I'd seen nothing like this straggling line of tiny low cottages, each with its garden that stretched toward the road behind a fence of weathered wooden pickets. I said, "These houses look old." Most were built of weathered gray logs, though here and there I saw a few splashes of yellow and blue paint.

"Probably built after the war," said Yasha.

I was disappointed. "Well, let's stop anyway." At least it was a village, like Streshin, not a maze of 12-storey apartment blocks.

"There may have been some houses here before the war, but if so, I'm sure they were destroyed." He pulled the Lada off the road and onto a straggling dirt track that led toward the village. It was deeply rutted and after driving a few yards he stopped the car.

"Too rough?" I said, and he nodded. "I wonder how the roads are around Streshin." I knew Yasha wasn't going to jeopardize his car. He'd already told me spare parts were unobtainable.

"I've been wondering, too."

Everyone got out of the car. We removed all our belongings, as we'd done at every stop. This time I decided to leave the liter of boiled water I'd been lugging around in a plastic cider bottle from Stockholm, which had a bright picture of an apple on the label. Valery leaned past me and covered the bottle with a newspaper. "It's only water," I said. "Why would anyone want to steal it?"

"For the bottle," he said. "It's foreign."

We walked up the dirt road. Roosters crowed and an unseen dog began to bark. The breeze carried the smell of pigs. There was no one in sight, but I knew we were being observed. I snapped some photographs. Most likely the inhabitants thought we were a government committee, come to hunt out infringements of the innumerable regulations that hemmed in the lives of ordinary citizens, and which Yasha had told me everyone broke continually because "it is the only way you can survive. And anyway, nobody is sure what is legal anymore."

Fenced in by pickets some distance from a house I saw an apple orchard consisting of five trees. The red, swollen fruit was ripe, and someone had propped a homemade wooden ladder against one of the trunks.

I walked in that direction, thinking about my great-grandfather. I'd never met him or seen his picture; I didn't even know his name. All I knew of him was the manner of his death, at least if the story my grandfather had told me was true. As a child, I'd accepted it. As an adult, there were details that puzzled me.

If he'd been killed by thieves while he was sleeping, presumably they'd have stolen the fruit that very night. They could hardly have taken days to do it or they'd have been caught. Yet, how could one or two men have picked so many apples in a single night? To me the word "orchard" conjured up hundreds of trees planted in rows, far from the nearest house, like the apple orchards of upstate New York or the orange

groves in Florida. How could a poor man (I knew he'd been poor), have afforded to rent such an orchard in the first place? And how, if he'd lived, would he have managed to pick all that fruit, carry it to market, and sell it?

Now I realized that the scale of his world must have been smaller than I, an American, had ever imagined; much, much smaller. It was for the sake of an orchard such as the one before me now that he had lost his life, plunging his wife and five children into a poverty so dire that they had been, as my grandfather once wrote to me in a letter, "hungry all the time."

The fruit had been ripe, just like these apples; the sudden attack—by whom? One assailant, or two?—had been savage and efficient, or the neighbors must have heard

cries. Perhaps they had, and ignored them; perhaps they knew what was happening and didn't care, or were bribed to keep silent with a cut of the profits. What difference did it make if there was one less Jew in the world?

By moonlight—yes, there had to have been moonlight—the thieves worked swiftly; by cock-crow they would have been gone. And not long after it was full daylight my grandfather came walking down the road, a boy of nine, carrying his father's breakfast in a pail.

I turned away. Two roughly dressed men had appeared out of nowhere, as if conjured up by my fantasies. They were staring at me, their eyes hot, their faces flushed. One of them was holding a bottle. They said something I couldn't understand.

Yasha saw them and came over at once, and he and the men exchanged a few words. They shambled off down the road in the direction of the Lada.

I asked, "What did they say?"

"Nothing. They are drunk."

Valery and Marina joined us, and we stood close together watching the men, who looked back at us over their shoulders. When they reached the car they paused, and then stumbled on.

Marina gave a sigh of relief. A blond boy of twelve or so darted out into the road, took a quick look at us, and retreated into a barnyard where chickens scratched in the dirt at the foot of a haystack.

I said, "I wonder what the houses are like inside."

Yasha said, "Do you want to see one? I can ask if someone will let us go in."

"Do you think that's a good idea?"

A barrel-chested man had appeared in the garden of a tiny house that looked like a child's drawing: a door in the middle, a window on either side, and a peaked roof through which a stub of chimney protruded. Yasha walked over and spoke to him.

"Pojalusta! Pojalusta!" the man cried. "Pojalusta"—the all-purpose Russian word that can mean "please", "thank you", or "excuse me." He was beaming and making sweeping gestures, indicating we were welcome to enter his house. We passed through the gate and into a kitchen garden as he continued speaking in hearty tones, addressing himself to me; I guessed that Yasha had told him I was an American. When I thanked him in English he laughed in a friendly way. He seemed about forty, and very energetic; he was wearing knitted sweatpants and a plaid shirt that barely closed around his girth.

From behind the front door, a little tow-haired girl peeped out at us. She took shelter behind his legs as he ushered us inside, explaining that the house was about thirty years old and had belonged to his mother. Recently she had died, and he was renovating it to use as a dacha. He was a truck driver, and lived in Minsk.

The house was about twenty feet square and almost empty of furniture. A living room and kitchen made up the older portion, and two small bedrooms had been added later. Tools lay about, and a window in the living room looked newly installed. Large glass jars of preserved tomatoes, cucumbers, and plums were stacked on the floor. "Da, da," he nodded, when I asked whether these came from the garden. He apologized because his wife was away in Minsk and therefore he couldn't offer me tea. With his permission I took his picture; it shows him smiling broadly and tucking in his shirt, which gapes to reveal his navel.

He invited me to inspect the massive stove, which occupied half the kitchen and stretched from floor to ceiling. It was made of brick, plastered and whitewashed, and jutted out into a shelf on which the family could sleep in winter. Not quite everything, I saw, had changed since my grandfather's day; or indeed since the sixteenth century, when Robert Burton had noted in his *Anatomy of Melancholy* that the Russians "live in stoves

Barnyard along the road.

and hothouses all winter."

When I touched the stove I found it pleasantly warm; curling slices of apple were spread out on the shelf to dry, in flat wicker trays. Our host told us he had built the stove himself without any plans, using traditional methods he'd learned as a boy by watching the older men.

"We were lucky with that man," remarked Valery, as we returned to the car.

Yasha gave the Lada a careful inspection, but it had not been tampered with. Since a thin rain had begun to fall while we were indoors, he took out a pair of windshield wiper blades and deftly attached them, explaining that he kept them in the trunk except when he was using them, so they wouldn't be stolen.

As we drove south toward Minsk, I thought about the house we'd just visited. How different was it, I wondered, from the one in which my grandfather had grown up? Not very, I was willing to bet. The stove had surely been similar; he'd spoken of sleeping on a stove in winter. Anyway, when simple people rebuild houses that have been destroyed, they try to duplicate the architecture they have known since childhood, which embodies for them the reassuring concept "house" and, closer to the heart, of "home."

We made one more stop on the way back to Minsk, at my request. Since Yasha had explained to me the importance of the dachas in the lives of Russian city-dwellers, I wanted to take a closer look at them.

The dachas we chose were clustered behind a wall not far from the road. To reach them we had to cross a narrow strip of land where small patches of potatoes, cucumbers, beets, and tomatoes were flourishing, despite the drought. They were being tended by several couples who glanced at us and quickly averted their heads.

"Does this land belong to the people in the dachas?" I asked Yasha.

"It belongs to nobody. Perhaps, to the kolkhoz. Wherever the people find a little land, they take it and grow vegetables."

Entering the gate, we strolled the dirt roads of the dacha community. Each house sat in its kitchen garden; each plot of land was small and of a uniform size, for government regulations had long limited the amount of land that could be privately owned, though this was now changing. No one looked at us or spoke. People's faces were closed; they seemed unwelcoming, even hostile. In every house, a curtain shifted in a window as we passed by.

I said, "In a small town in America, some of the people would say hello or nod as you walked down the street."

"They are afraid," said Valery. "Maybe they think we are government inspectors."

"Even now, with perestroika?"

"There is perestroika, but for how long? We have the habit of fear. These people are relatively well off. They have something to lose, something that can be taken away from them."

The houses were small, not much larger around than the one we'd visited in the village, but taller; two and three stories were piled on high cement foundations that enclosed garages and root cellars. The style of some of the houses amused Marina, especially one with rounded arches of light and dark brick. "From Italy," she commented, laughing.

Most of the dachas, though, were made of squared-off logs or weathered boards, like the houses I'd seen in the village, with similar windows and doors. The resemblance was no accident. A half-built dacha was being constructed of weathered logs with numbers painted on them, and Yasha said the logs must have come from a village house that had been abandoned. The logs had been numbered so they could be reassembled in the original order. It was cheaper to build this way than with new materials, and abandoned houses were not hard to find.

In the dacha community, just as in the village we had visited earlier, traces could be found of an older Russia, the Russia my grandfather had known, if I let myself perceive them. These traces went beyond objects that could been seen and touched, like a window of a certain size and shape, or the beets and potatoes swelling under the surface of the earth, to things equally pervasive, and deeper—the averted eyes, the fears, the hostility that buffeted me like a blow. Were these simply the legacy of Communism with its orthodoxies and myriad spies? Was that the whole story? I didn't think so. Surely the same emotions had tainted the air of Streshin when my grandfather had walked its streets, first as a child and then as a young man. Streshin's thirteen hundred Jews, oppressed by a harsh and bigoted regime and surrounded by a peasantry whose savagery was spurred on by a superstitious priesthood, had had much to lose, like the owners of these dachas: precious possessions that could be torn from them in the next pogrom, like a few bushels of apples, or the honor of a daughter, or even life itself. Strangers must have been watched, covertly and carefully, to see if they posed a threat.

I took Yasha, Marina, and Valery out to dinner at one of the best restaurants in town, in the reconstructed Old Quarter—the only restaurant that would admit us, incidentally. There were several others, but they'd all been reserved for wedding banquets. We saw a number of wedding parties—Saturday is a big wedding day because the registry office is open. Brides wear white, with flowers in their hair, and the friends form a procession in their cars which sport balloons and streamers, just as in the U. S. On the leading car, two white plastic swans were attached to the hood.

Dinner included a Belarusian specialty of wild mushrooms and sour cream that prompted Yasha to remark thoughtfully that only a short time ago we had been discussing the recent epidemic of wild mushroom poisonings—something I, too, had been thinking about but trying to repress.

"Perhaps, though, they are domesticated," said Yasha.

Valery said, "Yes, they must be domesticated. After all, six hundred people have been poisoned and ten percent have died. From mushrooms that looked perfectly harmless! They say the radiation may have caused a mutation—"

"Yes, these are surely domesticated."

Marina looked up. "They are wild." She sounded as if she knew what she was talking about, and we picked at them in silence.

This restaurant consisted of a large upstairs room. White tablecloths covered the tables, most of which were empty, perhaps because we'd come at an odd time, about 4:30 in the afternoon. The place was very smoky, and deafening American rap music was throbbing through the loudspeakers. The young people were very apologetic and asked me several times if this would do; if not, they were fully prepared to depart hungry. I assured them it was all right.

We had a large meal, not too bad. When the bill was presented it came to 460 rubles or about three dollars. My three guests watched with respect tinged with awe as I counted out eighteen 25-ruble notes and a ten, and paid the waiter. I do hope they enjoyed the outing, which was a rare treat for them. Marina generally cooks at home because it's cheaper. The food is better, too.

We discussed medical matters. Valery's mother is a physician. They asked me about medical care in the United States and how it is paid for, and I described the kind of medical insurance Joe and I have and what it covers. I also told them about some of the problems of health care: the poor using the emergency room as a family doctor, the poor who have no coverage at all, the AIDS epidemic, and the ever-increasing cost of medical care due in part to the development of high-tech health care. I described the logistics involved in obtaining a heart for a heart transplant, for example. They said there had been a tragic incident in a clinic not far from Moscow, where several dozen children, or more, had been infected with the AIDS virus by dirty hospital needles.

We talked about the size of families. They told me young people were having only one child or none at all. Because of "the situation," raising a child is just too difficult. Both Valery and his wife, and Yasha and Marina, have one child. I asked Valery if he would like to have more children. He said, "Probably, yes. One more child, if the situation was different. But now, no." They mentioned, as had the Ioffes, the precipitous fall in the birth rate, and the fact that it is now below the mortality rate.

I asked about the other patrons at the restaurant. What kind of people were these? There was a party of eight at one table, where a loud-voiced man held forth continually. What were they talking about? I explained that writers are shameless eavesdroppers, but since I didn't know Russian I was at a disadvantage.

Everybody obligingly listened. Valery said, "They are talking about a dog."

Later I asked again. This time Valery said, "It is a very stupid conversation. There are too many stupid conversations like that in Russia."

The loud man was saying, "Do you respect me or don't you respect me? Then why won't you drink with me?"

After dinner they dropped me off at the flat, where I took a nap. Then they picked me up and we all went to the home of Larisa Gazizova, the wife of Askhat Gazizov, who had exerted himself so heroically from Italy via e-mail on my behalf. Although I never actually met him, without his efforts as the "middleman" my trip would never have materialized. I wanted to thank him in some way, and I knew Larisa, too, had gone to some trouble to try and assist me, making phone calls and so forth; I wouldn't have felt right about leaving Minsk without meeting her and thanking her. I wanted to give her a gift of money, small by my standards but not by hers, even though her husband is abroad and will certainly bring back hard currency. I found some pretty notepaper and wrote her a note of appreciation in French, sealing it into an envelope with thirty dollars enclosed; a month and a half's salary. This I put in a plastic bag with some small gifts—chocolate, fancy soap, cigarettes, and stockings—which I planned to leave with her.

Language was the problem. She spoke no English. According to her husband, she spoke French, but when I met her she refused to say any more than "bonjour," insisting she couldn't. Unlike Marina, she never relaxed enough to try. I think her personal standards were too high for her to do anything less than well. Yasha and Valery were there to translate, so communication was possible though a certain formality persisted; she never stopped treating me like a Distinguished Foreign Guest.

She was older than the others, about forty, slim, blonde, chic, and rather sexy. She, too, was "half and half." There was a seventeen-year-old daughter who whisked herself into her room after snatching a glimpse of us, and a sweet nine-year-old who was studying English in school and shyly said, "How do you do?" and "It is very nice to meet you." An enormous young collie dashed excitedly around us, flinging himself on people and having to be dragged off repeatedly by Larisa, who seemed to weigh less than he did.

She showed us into the living room and shut the door to keep the dog out. A table had been opened up, and filled the center of the room. We sat down. There was some stilted conversation. Then Larisa began bringing out food, dish after dish, though I certainly hadn't expected anything but tea and perhaps cake. She must have emptied her larder of everything she had in the way of emergency rations, and spent the day preparing. She had produced a tuna salad, a dish of fried potatoes with mushrooms on top, a salad of cucumbers and tomatoes, a platter of cold tongue and pate beautifully arranged, a dish of ground cheese, garlic, and mayonnaise that must have left my breath very pungent but was delicious, bread and butter, a many-layered cake she had baked, and a bowl of fresh grapes that brought gasps from the others. "Grapes!"

"Oh yes," she lied gallantly. "I just happened to see them. They were very cheap."

Everyone stared at the food with amazement and deep respect. Valery said, "Our Belarusian women, they are miracle workers."

I said, "I see that. Larisa, you shouldn't have. This is just beautiful."

Valery translated, and she gave a slight smile and shrugged. She held her head very high on a slim, slender neck, and only a few times met my eyes with quick, darting glances.

I made a formal speech of appreciation to her and Askhat, which was translated and acknowledged with a regal nod. I got the unmistakable impression that she was a remarkable woman; despite the blonde fragility, her presence radiated forcefulness. I very much regretted my inability to speak to her except through an intermediary. Yasha told me later that she was an engineer, the head of a large division in some sort of heavy construction work, an unusual job for a woman. He said he found her "very interesting," because she had a strong character and also because although she was forty she was very—he hesitated, looking for the right word.

"Attractive?"

"Attractive, yes. It is very unusual. At her age, most Russian women do not keep themselves like that."

I could see I was expected to hold forth, and I did my best to rise to the occasion although it's not a role I'm comfortable with for long. It seemed I'd been doing this a lot since coming to Russia, probably giving people a false impression of myself. The conversation had a certain formality, without the easy give and take I'd enjoyed earlier in the day at the noisy restaurant.

I tried to answer everyone's questions about life in America. Did workers receive a pension when they retired? Were there any black people in the middle class? Didn't American politicians have exceptionally high moral standards in their personal lives? Were my books like those of Agatha Christie?

Like the others, Larisa had never seen an American in Minsk; in fact, I don't think she'd seen an American, period. Like them, too, she'd never heard of Streshin and wondered why I wanted to go there.

My grandfather had been born there, I said, and launched into the story I'd so often heard as a child, of how he had come to America.

"It was in 1905. My grandfather Meyer was a carpenter, twenty-one years old. It was a time of pogroms, as you probably know, a bad time, and thousands of Jews were immigrating to America. My grandfather wasn't eager to leave. He had a widowed mother to support, and a wife who was expecting a baby.

"Then he was notified that he was going to be drafted into the army. At that time he'd have had to serve for something like nine years, and many Jews were sent to Siberia, where they got sick and died. He decided he would serve his time in the army unless he was to be sent to Siberia, in which case he would try to escape. He soon found out he would have to go to Siberia.

"Apparently there was a law at the time that if a conscript ran away, his family would have to pay a large fine. However, if he escaped after he was already in the custody of the army, there was no fine; it was considered the army's responsibility to hold on to him.

"He was drafted and marched with his unit onto a troupe train heading north. Somehow he managed to jump off the train, walk across Russia, end up at a seaport, and sail to America. He landed in New York with three rubles in his pocket and his carpentry tools, started walking, saw a man with a horse and wagon who looked like a Jew, and spoke to him in Yiddish. This man gave him a ride to where a butcher who came from Streshin was living, and for a while he lived in this man's cellar. That was how he got started."

Larisa said, "What happened to his wife and the baby?"

"After a while he sent for them."

"How did he do that?"

I wondered if she wanted to emigrate. "He got a job and saved money," I explained. "Then he bought a ticket for his wife and child and sent it to them."

Valery said with a laugh, "The way Yasha will send for Marina and Olga."

Nobody picked up on this remark. Yasha was looking serious. He said, "This morning I called the synagogue in Minsk to ask about burial records. I thought we might be able to find the grave of your great-grandmother, Dorothy."

"What did they say? Any luck?"

"Unfortunately not. They told me to call a certain man, he had all the records." He stopped.

"Were you able to reach him?"

"Yes. We spoke. I told him what I wanted. He said, 'How much will you pay?'" Yasha sounded shocked; he spoke in a hushed tone. "I said, 'Nothing. I will pay nothing.'" There was a silence. I wondered how much the man had wanted. Probably only a couple of dollars. Yasha repeated stiffly, "I told him, 'I will pay nothing,' and he said, 'Then go find it yourself.'" Yasha looked at me, waiting for my reaction. Nobody spoke.

I felt a momentary irritation. Why hadn't Yasha told me sooner? Shouldn't it have been my decision, whether or not I wanted to pay for this piece of information? He was watching me steadily. I'm not as idealistic as him, I thought. The high moral tone doesn't come naturally to me. Does that make me a materialistic American who thinks she can buy anything? Or just Meyer Hankin's granddaughter, and god knows he taught us to value money, overvalue it, probably.

My grandfather, Max Hankin, at 17.

Was it important to me to find Esther Basia's grave? No, I realized. It hadn't been my idea to look for it. If I happened upon it, fine. I would take a picture and show it to the children. Perhaps I would feel something, perhaps not. I might not know what I was looking for, but I doubted it was a grave. Anyway, the living are more important than the dead, and I'd rather use the money to help Yasha come to America than give it to the ghoul he'd talked to on the phone. Not that it was an either/or matter.

Maybe Yasha was a bit of a prig, but if so I liked him for it.

When I left Larisa's, I took away with me the plastic bag I'd brought to give her. The contents didn't seem good enough. I wished I'd bought a few more boxes of nice chocolates from the duty-free shop, but I didn't have room in my suitcase. These people have a lot of pride, and although they need everything, it's very difficult for them to accept anything.

As it would be for me, if I were in their situation. As it had been for me to accept Larisa's helpfulness without feeling I had to repay her immediately.

Now I feel more in her debt than before.

That's probably how she would prefer it.

Yasha, Marina, and Valery dropped me off at the flat. I was sorry to say goodbye to Marina and to Valery. I've grown amazingly attached to these young people in one day. I kissed Marina and told her I was sorry she wasn't coming with us to Gomel; she has to stay in Minsk so she can cook for her bedridden grandmother. I told her, "I'll see you in America."

She sighed and shook her head. "I don't think that will happen."

I shook hands with Valery, whom I had liked enormously. He is soon going to Germany, where he has a two-year position—a great opportunity.

Yasha informs me that the problem of where I am to sleep in Gomel has been solved; Yeva, an old army comrade of his father's, has agreed to put me up in her flat. She has three rooms. It sounds perfect. I ask Yasha where he will be staying.

"Unfortunately, I think I will be sleeping in my car."

"Oh, no! Isn't there room for you in the apartment?"

"I think so, yes."

"Then why don't you stay there, too?"

"Maybe," he said. "We will see. I do not know a safe place to park in Gomel. One time near Smolensk, thieves broke into my father's car. They smashed the window and stole what was inside."

V. On the Road to Shreshin

Yasha showed up at the apartment at ten o'clock sharp for the drive south, but reported that he'd been unable to get gas at the two gas stations he'd tried, which he said was very unusual. His car uses a special gas, higher octane than normal or something.

We tried a third gas station on the outskirts of Minsk. There were five or six battered, very old-fashioned pumps. At three of them were short queues of elderly vehicles; but the pump with the kind of gas we needed was empty. So we proceeded to Yasha's private garage not far away, sort of a storage locker, one of dozens in a series of long rows, where he keeps his car during the winter. The garage used to belong to his late father, and now it's his. Inside were stored sheets of plywood, odds and ends of furniture, empty gas tanks, and one large canister that was full of gas. He often has to buy gas on the black market because his monthly ration of eight liters doesn't even provide enough gas to get to and from the dacha.

He hauled out the canister and prepared to fill an empty tank he had in the trunk of his car. He balanced a pink plastic funnel on top, and when I offered to steady it he said, "No, no, you must not, you will get gas on your hands, you will not smell delicious." I didn't insist, but as he struggled to lift the heavy canister and rest the lip against the funnel, it soon became clear that he needed assistance; so I simply held on to the funnel as he apologized profusely. When the can was full he stowed it in the trunk. Then he siphoned some gas from the canister into the gas tank of the car, and put the canister with the remainder of the gas back into the garage and snapped the padlock shut.

There were half a dozen men around, doing something to a truck, and drinking. Far down the aisle between the garages, an old car was propped at an angle, its two left wheels off the ground. Two men were working on it. A masculine world, this one.

I washed my hands, using the boiled water I always carried in a plastic liter bottle, and a sprinkle of the laundry detergent I brought with me in a baggie. I poured a little water into Yasha's hands, ignoring his protests, and rubbed my hand lightly on his so that he, too, would have soap.

Old buildings in Bobruisk.

We started south. I fed him bits of knekkebrod spread with peanut butter, which to my surprise he pronounced "delicious." I always assume only Americans appreciate peanut butter.

Bobruisk. August 23. We're in Bobruisk. I remember hearing my grandfather mention it when I was a child. According to Boris's encyclopedia, the population in 1897 was 35,000, more than half Jewish. All trade was in the hands of Jews at that time. The city was an important harbor on the Dnieper, and imported bread and salt. There were 22 factories employing 350 workers, two hospitals, one of them a Jewish hospital, and several schools including one church school. Much to my surprise we found a whole small district of old brick houses with fanciful moldings around the windows and doors and under the roofs. There was what must have been a main street of shops, two-story buildings, some of them with balconies above that made me think of people coming out on them, women, to see what was going on below; I remember the way my grandmother used to sit for hours at the window with her arms resting on the sill, watching what was going on in the street. Or maybe a young girl glimpsed on a balcony by my grandfather—Romeo and Juliet. Some balconies were enclosed in arches of stone. Yasha and I walked for several blocks, taking pictures.

In the same district there were two rows of old houses at right angles fronting on a very large square that is now planted as a park; it might well have been a square in the old days. The roofs of some of the houses were of metal—not corrugated but of panels, maybe bronze, they were blackish; the seams were crimped and folded over to shed the rain, just as in Stockholm where a saw a man demonstrating this old craft.

The road crossed the Berezina at Bobruisk. It wasn't very impressive, but Yasha tells me it floods all the low-lying land in the spring. It has a somewhat swampy look. There are some low wooden houses near the river, like a small village; he thinks it may go back to somewhere between the first and second world wars. They resemble the village house we visited but are somewhat larger and the roofs in this area have a peculiar dropped line at the front and back, instead of a plain gable end. No doubt this architectural feature has a name but I don't know it. The houses have touches of originality and personal expression, fanciful fretwork outlines the windows, gingerbread touches are here and there with considerable variety from one house to the next. I would guess many of these are traditional patterns that have been repeated in more modern houses. I imagined my grandfather travelling to Bobruisk from his village and being impressed by these houses and the brick buildings downtown, seeing them as wealthy and sophisticated.

Zlobin. We've just turned left on the road to Zlobin and Gomel. We passed a wooden, horse-drawn cart a moment ago, driven by a man who looked like a farmer. Inside the cart, a woman reclined on blankets. The cart was very simple, just a narrow floor formed by a board or two, and two sides slanting upward in a vee, each side formed by two horizontal boards.

The land is very flat. The road stretches away perfectly straight, with only an occasional slight incline. Here and there I see young oak trees that seem to have been planted.

Many of the village houses are basically log cabins. The logs are squared off and notched at the ends so that they overlap like Lincoln Logs.

We're in Zlobin district now, though we can't yet see the city. The land is flatter than ever, almost perfectly flat now. It stretches away to a distant horizon. Fields of corn are withering for lack of rain. Trees have been planted alongside the road. In the distance, a line of forest is dark against the sky. A few fires were smoldering on the outskirts of Minsk, but since we passed them we've seen no more fire or smoke. It's a warm day, almost hot. A few clouds in the sky; a haze in the air. Maybe that is smoke and pollution. We drive along an avenue between white birches. We pass an old-fashioned yellow bus with rounded corners. Through the grimy windows we can see that it is packed full of people standing, the standard way of travel, says Yasha.

A horse-drawn cart loaded with a mountain of hay stands at the side of the road, waiting for us to pass. A small blond boy sits on top of the hay.

We've just passed another horse-drawn cart, of the same triangular design I noticed before. It's the fourth I've seen in my trip.

Yasha tells me about "potato season," a few days in September when city-dwellers go out to the villages where their parents live to help them harvest the potatoes. Then everyone goes back to the city with bags of potatoes. Potatoes are sometimes called "the bread of Belarus."

We're on the outskirts of Zlobin, passing small, fenced village houses of different colors. Here's one of mustard yellow with blue trim; here's one that's green with brown trim. Behind them loom these huge, faceless, soulless, barren monoliths of new cement apartment buildings. Zlobin is smaller than Bobruisk, and the wooden houses here are simpler, with less ornamentation, and no gingerbread around the windows.

This was a market town of 2100 people back in 1902, more than half of them Jews, according to Boris's encyclopedia. Lumber used to go down the Dnieper through Zlobin to the Black Sea. Back then there was a church and a Christian school. We'll try to find the downtown, look around, and then head south to Streshin. It's three in the afternoon.

Nearing Streshin. We're only nine kilometers from Streshin now. I have a strange feeling. The road is narrower but adequate. The fields are full of people, barefoot, heavy-set women in babushkas, and bare-chested men with battered hats. The people here seem closer to the soil. They have the look of peasants. In the tiny gardens behind the houses, gardens are lovingly tended and thriving despite the drought.

Now we're passing a brand-new agricultural village. Many of the women wear head-scarves despite the heat. Yasha says some of the people from the nuclear zone around Chernobyl, fifty miles away, have been moved to this area, and the houses built for them.

Entering Streshin.

In the fields the stubble is golden. The haystacks crouch in a line like patient beasts.

The plowed earth is a soft brown, and powdery. We are passing apple orchards, the trees planted in straight lines and looking well-tended and pruned. Sheep browse the stubble by the side of the road, tethered to stakes. Some haystacks are long, like houses; others are conical, with pointed roofs.

We reached Streshin late in the afternoon. The village is a large one, with a reconstructed church. A man and a boy were cutting hay with long-handled scythes along the roadside. A horse-drawn cart passed, loaded with lumpy sacks containing potatoes, proceeded slowly down the dirt road. We raised a cloud of dust as we drove along.

The sign on the roadway, "Streshin," is battered and dented. We stop at Yasha's suggestion, and he takes my picture beside it. We enter the town, between small houses. Yasha says some of them are very old, unlike most of the houses we've seen

Old houses in Streshin.

elsewhere, which were built or rebuilt after the war.

We saw a cemetery containing crosses and I said, "I wonder if there's a Jewish cemetery."

Yasha said, "I will ask." A man in grey workman's clothes and a stubble of grey beard

Old cemetery and eroded gravestone.

was walking down the street in our direction. Yasha stopped the car, got out, and had a conversation with him. Then he opened the back door and invited the man inside saying, "He will show us the way."

The man got in. He said there were only a few Jews left in town, and he knew them.

We turned off the road onto a track that led out into the fields, as Yasha reeled off the names of some of my relatives. Did he know the names Raskin and Gorelick?

"Da, da," he said. Yes, he knew them. Raskin was my grandmother's maiden name. The cemetery used to be over there, he indicated. There was nothing to be seen but long grasses and a grove of birch trees. We got out of the car and walked to where the cemetery had been. The ground was lumpy and rutted under the matted weeds. I found one headstone, half-buried and overgrown, and took a picture of it while Yasha talked with the man some distance away.

Below the knoll where we were standing coiled the Berezina; some distance away, long fingers of woodland stretched toward the water through golden fields.

The man said he was fifty-seven and had been a child at the time of the war, and didn't remember much. There was a Jewish man named Raskin who worked in town, he said; he knew him quite well, because they'd been classmates in school.

I told Yasha to tell the man that we were almost the same age, and that if my grandfather hadn't gone to America, and I had grown up in Russia and survived the war, that he and I might have been classmates, too.

He said he knew a Jewish family living in Streshin and would take us to their house.

Yasha with our guide.

We drove through Streshin, between rows of brightly painted houses—yellow, blue, red, and green, bright, naive peasant colors like those on the Dimka terracotta ware that Nina Ioffe is so fond of. Each house was protected by a wooden wall with a gate; there were sheds and outbuildings behind the walls. Roosters crowed and I smelled pigs and manure. Conical haystacks indicated the presence of livestock in some of the courtyards, perhaps a cow, though I didn't see any, or a horse.

Top: The Goldin's House. Below: A painted house in Streshin.

We stopped before a wooden house with battered blue shutters. The house was unpainted, and had weathered and darkened with age. We knocked at the high gate.

A heavyset old woman with brawny arms opened the gate a crack and peered out at us blankly. She had a straggle of long, greasy dark hair streaked with gray. After some conversation in Russian she began to smile. There were no teeth in the front of her mouth, except for one or two gold ones that hung crookedly on the sides. Her skin was coarse, her body shapeless in a soiled cotton housedress. Something in me recoiled but I tried to ignore it. She waved us in with some warmth, and placed her arm around my waist for a moment as she drew me inside.

We entered a tiny courtyard entirely filled with clotheslines on which bedding had been hung to air, puffy down comforters and pillows. Large white chickens scratched in the corners.

"Avram! Avram!" she called, as we passed through the tiny kitchen into a dark living room that wasn't much bigger. The place smelled of mildew and bad drains, and when Yasha and I took a seat, at her urging, at a table covered with a threadbare red velvet cloth, the chair cushion and the cloth on which I placed my hands felt damp.

Avram, like his wife, was in his seventies. He had a mischievous, somewhat sly smile, a long nose, and gleaming false teeth.

Both of them were amazed that I had come from America, although the woman told me some years back a man from Chicago had also come to Streshin to see the place

Rosa and Avram Goldin.

Left: Bedding airing in courtyard. Right: The Goldin's living room.

where his ancestors had come from.

Our hosts were named Rosa and Avram Goldin. We repeated the litany of names—by this time the man who had led us there had vanished. They nodded when I said "Gorelick" and Rosa told me her mother had been a Gorelick. There had been many Gorelicks in that area. Of course most of the Jews who had remained in Streshin during the war had been killed, but she and her husband had managed to survive by fleeing to the Urals. They were now the only Jewish family in Streshin; they had returned after the war to care for her elderly mother, who was there alone after her husband had been killed by the Nazis.

`Now Rosa worked in a shop, one of the very few in town, although she was seventy-four. It was impossible for her to quit because the times were so hard and they needed the money. Her husband, who had had to retire, now took care of the house. He made us some tea, and Rosa insisted we eat. She fried us eggs in a pan full of bubbling fat. I realized these people must depend a great deal on the eggs from their chickens to survive.

Avram had been a teacher, and there were books in every room of the house. The house consisted of a living room about 10x12, two tiny bedrooms, a small kitchen, another room whose purpose wasn't clear to me that was separated by a partition from another, tiny room that was almost completely filled by a huge tiled Russian stove with a ladder propped against the side; the couple slept on it during the winter. The house was a hundred years old, they told us, and although it had had some renovations, no great changes had been made. They'd bought it from another Jewish family who had lived there; their own house had been destroyed during the war.

Both Rosa and Avram were still very sharp-witted and seemed energetic, despite the hardships of their life. Rosa wept as she spoke of the destruction of the Jewish population, and Avram told us with indignation that the Jewish cemetery we had visited had been destroyed by bulldozers only this spring. They'd come in and just plowed the whole thing up. He had protested strongly to the mayor, and as a result the destruction was slightly less than total.

Rosa had a brother in America; he went to Philadelphia to live and then moved, she thinks, to New York. She gave me his name and that of his son and asked me to try and find them. She lost contact with them during the Stalinist period, when it was dangerous to receive letters from America. Another relative, a man who must now be 99 if he is still living, had emigrated and come back once to Streshin for a visit many years ago. Avram wrote down the names and addresses, as far as they knew them, and I promised to try and look them up. I told Rosa it was unlikely I would find them, as the names were very common. The brother who may live in New York was named Abraham Spiva.

Avram rather delightedly kept bringing out folders of old letters and papers and documents, and books, and showing them to us, reminding me of Joe's father, who'd loved to do the same thing. These are indeed the people of the Book, even in this tiny, primitive village.

Avram and Rosa Goldin.

The eggs were excellent, and so was the bread and butter. Incautiously, I ate a piece of salami and some sliced tomatoes from their garden. Probably it was one or the other that made me sick. I'd watched Rosa washing the tomatoes in water from a pail on the kitchen counter. She poured water from the pail into a chipped enamel basin, dumped in half a dozen tomatoes, and quickly rolled them around in the water, a timeless gesture. The house had no running water; water had to be brought from communal pumps out by the

Avram Goldin.

road. There was no water, they told us, due to the drought. It hadn't rained all summer. There was very little water even in the central water station in town. They were worried about this, understandably. No wonder Rosa's dress was dirty and her hair unwashed.

They have a married daughter and grandchildren in Israel. A married son in Leningrad was unable to emigrate because he was married to a Russian woman. It was bad, they said, to be separated from their children.

When they heard the name "Hankin", my grandfather's name, they shook their heads. Could we mean "Gonkin?" I said I didn't know. Rosa said a woman of that family lived in Zlobin. I said I didn't think that anyone was still alive, but when they told me she was the daughter of a man named Mendel I said, "My grandfather had a brother named Mendel who stayed in Russia. All the other siblings came to America."

They became very excited. "Yes, yes, she is his daughter, her name is Zina. Zelda."

"My mother's name was Zelda. If this woman is really the daughter of my grandfather's brother Mendel, then she would have been my mother's first cousin. Perhaps they were both named after the same deceased relative."

Rosa said that Zina used to receive letters from an uncle who had gone to America. "Yes," I said. "I remember my grandfather getting letters in Yiddish from Russia."

"And she used to get packages."

"My grandmother used to send packages. Clothing."

She nodded vigorously. Yes, yes, clothing, they sent clothing, it must be the same woman.

Avram telephoned Zina in Zlobin and had a conversation with her that made Yasha and Rosa smile. He seemed to be repeating the same things over and over again. He hung up, shaking his head, and said, "She is old." She was confused, and he hadn't managed to convey much information to her.

However, she did live in Zlobin, to which we were about to return so we could get on the road to Gomel, where we're spending the night. Yasha wrote down her address.

We left after I presented them with a bag containing a few small gifts and twenty dollars in American money, which to them is a large amount. I gave them these things

Rosa Goldin.

in a bag which they were to open after my departure. Rosa begged me to write her a letter and I said I would.

As I was leaving the Goldins' house, Rosa came and stood very close to me, gazing into my eyes. She laid her palms on the slope of my breasts, a curiously touching and childlike gesture, and spoke to me long and earnestly, thanking me for my visit and asking me to be sure to write her a letter from America.

This experience was so intense, in that tiny house which must have been exactly like the one where my grandfather grew up, that I was too overwhelmed to want to drive much around the town or look at the landscape—which I wish now I'd done. I regretted, too, that the Russian man who'd led us to the Goldins had slipped away before I had a chance to give him the pack of cigarettes I had in my pocket. When I went to look for him, he was gone. In the car he had apologized because he'd been drinking, which he'd never have done if he'd known we were

Saying good-bye.

coming. I assured him it was all right. In fact, he wasn't noticeably drunk.

Everyone has been apologizing to me since my arrival—for being unprepared for my visit, for not giving me finer food, for not being dressed in their best clothes.

We looked for the road out of Streshin and then saw the reconstructed church, gleaming, all white rounded apses and golden domes.

I asked Yasha to drive over to it, which he very patiently did. He has been angelic. Without his help, none of this would have been possible. He is fearless about going up to people and asking questions, and finding his way to obscure places.

We stopped near the church and walked up a dirt road and I took a picture of it. It is unexpectedly grand for a small country town. I hadn't expected it to be so beautiful. If I ever go back to Streshin I'd like to walk around the church and go inside. Most incongruously, loud western dance music was pulsating through the air. I couldn't imagine why, but as I neared the church I saw, off to one side, a young blond woman dancing in a courtyard with a tiny child. I stood there in amazement, watching her. She danced on and on, rocking and rolling and shaking her hips, as the child stumblingly tried to imitate her, waving its tiny arms and looking about to tumble into the dust. I thought, "So there is life in Streshin."

I snapped a picture of the two of them, and then another. I am aware of Yasha, stiff as a sentry, watching me watch them. The woman seems lost in her dance, but suddenly as she whirls she catches sight of us, stops, and after a moment comes out to where we stand. She looks about thirty, with frizzed, bleached-blond hair, heavy blue eye shadow, a short, tight, denim skirt, and a see-through blouse trimmed with lace. She

Streshin Church of the Intercession of the Holy Virgin.

seems totally unlike anyone I've seen in Streshin.

Yasha tells her I've come from America, and she looks at him skeptically. "From America? You're kidding. Is she really?" Up close there is something world-weary about her; she is older than I thought. The loud music is still throbbing through the air. I feel a desire to make contact with her, directly. I wish I could talk to her, but that's impossible, so I reach out my hand. She takes it immediately. We look into each other's eyes. After a moment we find ourselves swaying to the music. Both of us laughing, we begin to dance, she in her tight denim skirt and sexy blouse, I in my travel-creased shirt and baggy pants, with my camera dangling from one hand and my WETA tote bag in the other. As the American music pounds and swells in the long shadow of the church, our dance grows faster and faster, a dance of reaching across miles, across years, across differences that are

The dancing woman.

unfathomable; a dance of survival and joy, as when Miriam and her women danced with their timbrels along the shore of the Red Sea.

As we drove out of Streshin Yasha said, "You are happy? You enjoyed your visit?"

"Yes, very happy. It was incredible. Extraordinary. I never expected anything like this. What an amazing adventure!"

"Oh? You are having an adventure?"

"Of course, an adventure. And you? Are you having an adventure, too?"

"Me? No. This is my country. For me, this is not new. For me an adventure is to go to a different country."

"You mean, meeting me doesn't count as an adventure?"

He looked at me but didn't answer.

VI. Zina

I was very tired. Nevertheless, when we reached Zlobin we decided to try and find the daughter of Mendel Gonkin. She lived on a street called "International," which no one seemed to have heard of. We drove around and around the battered cement apartment buildings that make up most of Zlobin. The people we spoke to seemed unfriendly. Closed and suspicious. Their faces struck me as mean and rather stupid.

After half a dozen attempts to find the street, Yasha stopped the car and asked two young women who were standing on a corner. They shrugged. They hadn't heard of International Street. They hurried away. We turned the corner and drove down a street of tiny wooden houses like the ones in Streshin. To our amazement there was a sign on one of the houses, the first street sign we'd seen in Zlobin; this narrow dirt track was International Street and the house was number 29. The house we were seeking was number 17.

We parked in front of one of the small houses. There were two women outside, and two children. The women looked tough, sullen, and brutish. One in particular had a sinister, ferrety face. They made no move in our direction as we got out of the car. Two nearly naked children, who looked half-starved and imbecilic, stared at us vacantly. The ferrety woman raised her hand and I saw that a knife had appeared in it, an eight-inch kitchen knife that was dented but sharp.

Yasha addressed the other woman, asking if she knew where Zina Markovna lived.

"In the back." The house was divided in two, and Zina lived in the rear.

All the while, the woman with the knife stared at us menacingly. I passed close to her as we walked into the courtyard. I smiled at her and nodded. After a moment she responded with a curt nod.

Over a low fence at the far side of the courtyard we saw her, a stooped old woman with a kerchief covering her hair, standing with her back to us. She heard us and turned, and for a moment I reeled as she gazed at me out of the eyes of my dead mother. It was

First cousins: Zina Markovna (l) and my mother (r).

a fleeting impression and never returned, for her features and my mother's were quite different, except for the eyes; yet from that moment I had no doubt that I had found my family.

She had been expecting us, and ushered us into a house that was even smaller than that of the Goldins, with fewer possessions, although there were some books. Before her retirement, Zina had been a teacher. She was agitated. She had a tragic face; all the lines around her mouth dragged downward. Her eyes had a haunted look. She couldn't sit still, but kept jumping up and moving around. But she wasn't senile, just depressed and, at the moment, overwhelmed by my arrival. She couldn't stop touching me, clasping my hands and hugging me. She asked if I knew the name of my great-grandmother.

I said, "Esther Basia."

"Esther Basia! Esther Basia!" she screamed. "She knows the name of Esther Ba-

Esther Basia, 1910

sia! She is Uncle Meyer's grandchild!" Gazing deeply into my eyes she wailed, "Help my son immigrate to America!" Then she dragged me over to a cupboard crying, "Uncle Meyer! Uncle Meyer! Meyer was the oldest, the head of the family!" She kept saying it over and over. With trembling hands she took out a pair of ancient, blackened scissors about sixteen inches long. These were the first thing Meyer had sent his brother Mendel from America, because Mendel was a tailor and needed a good pair of scissors.

How this battered relic managed to survive the war, I can't imagine. All of my grandfather's letters are gone, of course, together with most of her possessions and those of her late husband.

She told me that Esther Basia had been a very fine cook, and whenever there was a wedding it was she who would bake the wedding cake. Then she mentioned that Esther Basia's husband had been killed in an orchard—did I know?

Yasha told her I did and said to me, "The story you heard is true, then."

I asked the name of my great-grandfather, which I'd never known. She said he was called Simche Yoshi Gonkin.

Within moments, a stout old woman, cheerful and much more vigorous, appeared at the door. She said Zina had been her son's teacher many years ago, and that the two of them were good friends and saw each other every day. This neighbor, whose name was Mira, was immigrating to Israel soon. I thought about what a loss this would be for Zina.

Zina kept talking incessantly, so fast that it was hard for Yasha to keep up with what she was saying. We sat down and she poured us tea, and brought out bread and butter and a bowl of strawberry jam, all she had to offer. She seemed desperately poor. She was reeling off the names of my grandfather's sisters: "He had a sister named Risha—and a sister named Dosha—and a sister named Mary..."

I couldn't believe I was hearing the names of my great-aunts, these women I hadn't seen since childhood, all now dead, uttered in this poverty-stricken hovel so many thousands of miles from Brooklyn. At the sound of these names, spoken here, deep in Belarus, tears sprang into my eyes. We clutched each other, we hugged, we kissed, we wept. I've never had such a feeling.

My great aunts.

She spoke of hardships during the war, terrible times, of people who had died, of the sufferings of the Jews. Of prices that rise every month, threatening the tiny pittances they have. Of the constant fear that they will be unable to survive.

I said in an undertone to Yasha, who was sitting beside me, "What can I do for this woman? She's desperately poor."

He said, "May I be frank with you? You can do nothing for her, except help her son immigrate to America."

She spoke of a memorial that has recently been erected to the martyred Jews of Streshin, Zlobin, and Gomel. I don't know where it is, or whether I can bear to go there.

Zina's son, she told us, was named Boris. He was an engineer and lived in Gomel, where we were to spend the night. She telephoned him and excitedly told him of my arrival, and Yasha said, "Her son wants to know how old you are."

I thought, uh oh, I guess a rich American wife would come in handy, and said, "Tell

Left, Mendel Gonkin in 1918 and, right, after World War II.

him I'm married."

I had nothing to give her, and didn't want to go out and start rooting around in the car under the eye of her sinister neighbors. I was afraid this might somehow jeopardize her. So I gave her 400 rubles in 25-ruble notes, and a few dollar bills that happened to be loose in my pocket, explaining that I would have liked to bring her a lovely present but hadn't known of her existence.

"No! No!" she cried, pushing away the money. "Nothing for me! Only for my son!"

"Da, da," I murmured, embracing her and slipping the notes into the pocket of her sweater.

I said I had to go. She grew very still, gazing into my eyes as if memorizing my features, and laid her hands on my breasts as Rosa Goldin had done. She said, "You are a brave woman."

The car was still where we had left it, and undamaged. I got inside and leaned across

Zina's house: Inside (left) and back yard (right).

to open the lock on Yasha's door. As we drove away he said, "It could be dangerous for her to give her money." I didn't reply, but I realized with a terrible pang that he was right. But there was nothing to be done now. I'd given her only about five dollars in all, but I wished it had been in five and ten ruble notes instead of twenty-fives, although they are worth less than a quarter. I could only hope they wouldn't call attention to the fact that she might have a bit of money in the house.

I said, "One of those women had a knife. Did you see?"

"Yes. I saw."

Dorothy with Zina.

VII. Gomel

It was eight o'clock and growing dark as we hunted for the road to Gomel, which was an hour and a half away. I was mentally and physically exhausted, and hoped that when we reached Yeva's apartment it wouldn't be necessary to have a long conversation. I wanted to go straight to bed. Yasha kept asking people for directions and eventually found the right road.

We drove southeast in silence as the last pale strip of daylight clung to the western horizon. There were few cars on the road. The fields came right up to the road, and stretched far away in perfect flatness. We saw no woodlands now. The few scattered houses were so distant they could barely be glimpsed.

After a while Yasha said, "My grandmother was murdered by her neighbors."

"By her neighbors?"

He nodded, his eyes straight ahead. "They broke into her house to steal. They took everything she had. They drowned her in the water closet."

He drove fast down the two-lane road, passing the few cars we saw. He said, "Soon it will be dark."

"I think when it's dark here, it will be really dark. No house lights. Certainly no street lights."

"Yes, it will be very dark. Another new experience for you, Dorothy."

I groaned. "I can't take any more new experiences. Not today. I've had enough."

Yasha said, with apologies in advance for perhaps being too personal, that the thing his wife had found most remarkable about me was my skin. She thought it amazing that I didn't have any lines. Actually of course I have some. She wanted to know how old I was and he said, "Maybe forty."

I laughed. "Add twenty, Yasha."

I wish he'd stop apologizing for all sorts of minor offenses he fears he has committed. I told him if I had a ruble for every time he's said he's sorry, I'd be a rich Russian. He laughed.

We drove in companionable silence, talking occasionally. I began thinking about my unknown cousin Boris, and wondering what I'd gotten myself into. I was beginning to feel it was more than I'd bargained for. I asked Yasha how people immigrated to America. He said it was difficult, though easier than before Gorbachev. There is a quota and the waiting list is long, but if a relative in America is willing to guarantee that the émigré won't become a financial drain, things go more quickly, as they do if the émigré can afford to buy a ticket. Otherwise an American Jewish relief organization will provide one, but after considerable delay.

I asked Yasha if he, himself, wanted to immigrate to America.

To my surprise, he said no, and that his friend Valery didn't, either. What both of them want is the opportunity to travel, to work for a time in a country where they can earn hard currency. But if perestroika had not come, he would undoubtedly have wanted to emigrate to America or Israel. Now, though, he has hope that things will get better, so he would rather stay here. Marina, he said, doesn't want to emigrate.

As we drove along in the dark, Yasha began to talk about Chernobyl. He said, "I was in my office at the Institute when one of my colleagues ran in, very excited, and said there had been an accident at the nuclear reactor at Chernobyl. A big explosion, a disaster. At first I didn't believe him. I turned on the radio, but there was no information. Then, little by little, I heard some information on the news, not much, only a sentence or two. It was true, there had been an explosion. There had been an accident. Of course they said it was all over and there was no danger, but that was a lie. It was still continuing.

"It so happened I had a very good, very accurate radiation dosimeter. My father, you understand, had been in the military. He was with a unit that was in charge of radiation control. You know the Russians did test some atomic bombs. I went home and got the dosimeter, and changed my clothes. I tested my hair. It was radioactive. I took a shower and washed my hair, but that did not help. So I cut off all my hair.

"When my daughter was born, I tested the milk for radiation, Marina's milk, but it was safe. And for the first year, I tested all her food before she would eat it.

"People are very worried about the radioactivity. Now it is safe. I am a physicist, I understand these things. Not in the forbidden zone around Chernobyl, of course. There, no one lives any more except a few old people who wish to die where they have always lived. But others have been relocated. New flats have been built for them. I tell people now that the food is safe, the water is safe. They do not believe me, but it is so. Of course, the long-range effects are not known.

"There was a very fine Institute of Health in the Soviet Union. They monitored these things, the health matters. But now of course it is destroyed. No one knows what is happening. The official reports I have seen. I checked the mathematics, and the calculations were wrong. Of course I am not an expert, but I could tell they were wrong.

"There are certain fish that were not safe to eat. Very dangerous. The radiation concentrates in these fish, a thousand times more than is safe.

"The people here are nervous, very nervous. The incidence of neurosis has become very high. Sixty percent more than in other parts of Russia."

Finally we arrived in Gomel. The city, the second largest in Belarus, was very dark; most of the street lights had been turned off to save electricity. The streets were full of people, walking or waiting at the bus stops where some of them tried to flag us down and get a lift. Yasha had no idea where Yeva's street was, and no map of Gomel. He kept stopping the car and asking people, and by using what I told him was the "method of successive approximations" we gradually got closer. Yasha did the same thing in Bobruisk and Zlobin, to my surprise and admiration. American men, my husband included, hate to ask directions; and since good maps are available, they don't often have to. I told Yasha I admired his indefatigability—in Gomel he must have stopped twenty times to ask the way—and he said they had a saying, "With my mouth I can get to Kiev."

Even Yasha got a bit worn down by the process of finding Yeva's flat though. When he got back in the car after one of our stops, I asked him, "Did they give you directions?"

He clutched his head. "Too many directions."

By the time we got to Yeva's apartment, he had a bad headache. I gave him a couple of Tylenol, which cleared it up in half an hour. He was very grateful and commented that it was "strong medicine."

Yeva had made us a dinner of boiled potatoes, tomatoes, cucumbers, and bread and butter, plus a can of mackerel. I ate and went straight to bed.

Monday, August 24, 1992. Yeva's apartment, Gomel—Visit to Boris. This morning, poor Yasha appeared with a crick in his neck after sleeping all night in the car. I wanted to rub it, but decided not to. A kind of intimacy has grown up between us, but it's better not to breach the physical boundary. But he's a dear, and I feel close to him.

We went over to the apartment of my cousin, Boris Markovich Asnin, in Gomel this morning. Boris kissed my hand; he smelled strongly of garlic. He is the son of Zina, whom we met yesterday. He's an engineer, 45, divorced from a Russian woman, with two children. One son is married and expecting a child and lives in another city. The daugh-

Cousin Boris.

ter, younger, lives with her mother. At the moment she is in Belgium visiting some people she met last year, when she was taken to Belgium for a summer vacation for children of Chernobyl. Boris is quite nice-looking, with a stocky but trim build, dark hair and eyes, and a moustache.

I wasn't feeling well; I had a slight fever and was in a cold sweat much of the time. My head and stomach felt terrible. Nonetheless they bombarded me with food—not so very insistently, actually Yeva has been worse. Every five minutes she asks me what I want to eat. She can't seem to accept that I'm ill and simply cannot eat to make her feel good.

We visited Boris's apartment and spent some time with him and his sister, Sofa (Sofia). Boris speaks some English, self-taught. He spoke for hours in broken English, which must have cost him quite an effort. It also required some concentration on my part. Now and then he would lapse into Russian, which Yasha would translate. Sofa is a nurse in a maternity hospital and speaks no English. Her son and daughter have both immigrated to New York City, and she is going to emigrate next year and join them.

I tried to tape our conversation, but the tape is very hard to hear. I won't try to transcribe much of it. Boris knows some English, which he taught himself, and he was amazingly persistent in trying to speak it; but it was a slow and sometimes painful business, though I think I found it more tiring than he did.

Boris: I think I am last branch of family. Last one. I am very happy to know I have family in America.

Dorothy: But you have a son and a daughter.

B: Yes, but their mother is Russian.

D: So they're half Jewish.

B: Half, yes.

Boris didn't remind me of anyone in the family, although he does resemble his mother. He said I reminded him of his grandfather, Mendel. He and Sofa seemed nice, but not very interesting. The visit dragged on and on. I felt there were hidden agendas—not even particularly hidden—about immigrating to America and my helping in some way. I asked if he wants to come to America. He said, not now, because he doesn't want to leave his mother. But when she dies, he'd like to come to America if he can. However, he'd like his son to come. His son is a sailor who happened to telephone during the visit and was very much surprised to hear that I was there. He immediately told Boris to tell me that if I could get him a job on a good ship, he would emigrate.

All this has made me uneasy. On the one hand, I would like to help these people to make a new life, if that's what they want. On the other, I don't particularly want to be deeply involved with them. I don't feel I have much in common with them—unlike my feeling about Yasha and Marina, whom I would gladly invite to stay in our house for an extended period, with Olga. But Boris seems very needy to me, somehow, and if we were to guarantee him in the States and he stayed with us, it would be quite a heavy burden because he would need not only financial support but transportation assistance and a lot of our time, since he'd be completely isolated out in the suburbs. We're going to be away on sabbatical and so forth, we travel a lot—really, it would be difficult for us to provide the kind of emotional support he might need.

He told me some stories of his childhood. He remembered his grandfather Mendel quite well. His mother used to take him to Streshin to visit his grandfather, which he enjoyed. He was fond of his grandfather, and since Boris was a city child, he used to love the smell of fresh hay, for example. There was a haystack in the back yard, and he used to climb on top and lie there. He also liked to sleep on the big stove.

For some reason, when he was a very young child he was afraid of his grandfather's pants! To frighten him and make him behave, his mother used to wave them in front of him; he would become so scared that he would run and hide behind the stove. Under the stove lived a chicken, and he liked to steal the eggs and suck them dry; then the grandparents would be very surprised when they went looking for an egg and there was nothing there.

Mendel was a tailor and very poor. Boris said, "His light was never out." He would sew late into the night. He made coats for private individuals. As he sat sewing he would sing in Yiddish a song about how hard the life of a tailor is, and how poor he is, and how he doesn't have anything to eat. Boris chuckled at this memory and sang a verse of the song.

Boris's grandparents kept a cow in the courtyard, and when he was thirsty he would go out and drink milk directly from the cow's udder. He would milk the cow into a cup, and drink the warm milk. (Even the thought of it, today, made me queasy!)

The visit went on and on. Physically I was very uncomfortable. The chairs were uncomfortable, my stomach hurt, yet I couldn't hurt their feelings by leaving—I felt myself in a heavy family morass, the first time since arriving in Russia I've felt this way. But it's a familiar feeling. Family is wonderful and also terrible. Suddenly I felt stickily enmeshed in that familial web of expectations and obligations and guilts, instead of just joyfully adventuring forth, as I do with Yasha. I was very happy to make it possible for him to come to America. When I left the money in his apartment I felt fine about it because it was a gift freely given, totally. This doesn't feel freely given. If I give something, more will be expected; and then more and more. Whenever I draw the line, no matter how much I've given, there will be resentment. Or so I feel. And I suspect my grandfather was often in this position with his poor relations. I remember he built a house for his sister Mary, "so she would have where to lay her head." But according to Mary's daughter, Shirley Yaeger, Mary resented all her life that it was such a small house! And Shirley thought her mother's attitude quite reasonable.

We toured the city with Boris and Sofa and visited a cathedral that was used during the Stalinist period as a planetarium, but is now being restored. Many candle flames were twinkling before gilded icons, and outside in the yard, workmen were reconstructing one of the smaller, side domes. I was interested in examining the wooden framework of the dome, to see how it is made. It will be covered with metal and then gilded. Behind the cathedral was a chapel of the princely family to whom all this land, Gomel and the surrounding area, was given as a gift by one of the Tsars. The chapel has an ungainly brick base, which is crowned by a brightly colored fantasy of domes of various sizes and shapes—quite delightful. A smaller brick building some distance away is the entrance to an underground tunnel leading to the chapel; the tunnel contains the tombs of the family.

We strolled through a cool, shady park with many benches. I would have enjoyed it more if I'd been feeling better, and I was not up to walking to see the famous view of the river, to Boris's disappointment. He would also have liked to show me a unique tree that had been brought from Siberia. This park dates back to the 18th Century, I think, and is the pride of Gomel. In it are several museums that were formerly the ducal home and the servants' quarters; these survived the wartime devastation.

We returned to Yeva's apartment, where I spent most of the afternoon and evening in bed.

August 24, continued; at Yeva's apartment in Gomel. Yeva is trying to kill me with kindness. When I refuse her offers of food, her face becomes a mask of tragedy. We communicate in German; I'm doing better than I thought I could, but it's exhausting.

Later. I've just had a long, good discussion with Yasha about the whole cousin emigrating question. I now realize that when Boris wants to come to America he'll be able to join his sister and niece and nephew in New York, he doesn't need me for that. And I will tell him that I'll buy him a ticket. When the time comes, he should have his niece and nephew get in touch with me and we'll work it out.

Yasha has gone out to spend a little time wandering around Gomel. I told him I'd like to spend a quiet evening at home, even though maybe I should go out and see more, since I'm going home tomorrow. But I'm ill. And I can't take in any more new experiences right now. It's as if you were to go to the well with a pail and then figure that, as long as you're at the well anyway, you should get more water; but the pail will only hold water up to the brim, and not a drop more. Right now, I feel like that pail.

I've just taken an activated charcoal pill given to me by Yeva, at Yasha's suggestion. Maybe it'll settle my stomach.

Incidentally, when I first told Yeva I wasn't feeling well, her first response was, "It must be the radioactivity."

She was here in Gomel during the accident at Chernobyl, and she never left the city. She must have received a heavy dose of radiation.

Yeva is going to Minsk tomorrow with Yasha, to buy a present for her granddaughter. I gave her forty dollars in American money, as rent for two nights. When we'd discussed it, she didn't want to take any money, and asked me not to tell Yasha, or give her the money when he was around; I complied. She felt dreadfully ashamed, saying, "I am a Jew and you are a Jew. You are like a sister to me. I would like you to stay here for nothing."

"I know you would," I said, and held her in my arms while she wept.

After a while she wiped her eyes. "Tell your children if they want to come to Gomel, they can stay with me and I will treat them like a mother."

Yeva is alone and seems lonely and very worried about money. She has no job. I don't know where her income comes from. In the bathroom there are three tubes of toothpaste that are open and the insides scraped until there is hardly even a trace of white on the metal; yet they haven't been thrown away. She would like to work and she's very qualified—she told me at great length that she'd attended military academy and flying school and had been a pilot; she has worked as a German translator and taught German in college. She was married for quite a few years although she said the marriage wasn't a happy one. "I am sixty-seven," she said. "I am old, but I have a young heart. I could love again, if I met a man, I'm not too old." She'd like very much to have a job but says no one will hire her; they say, "Why should we hire you when we can get someone younger?"

Her flat is comfortably furnished in an old-fashioned style. There's a china cabinet in the living room containing her prized crystal. The bedroom, which I am occupying, is decorated with a large poster of a fluffy white cat, a calendar picture of a sailing ship, and innumerable photos, many of them of Yeva in her younger days when she was, not beautiful, but a strong, attractive girl. A philodendron plant on the table has been trained along the top of the headboard of her bed; the ends twine around the wall lamp above my head.

While I was taking a nap this afternoon, Cousin Boris sent me a bouquet of roses, six red and one pink. Yeva put them in water and they are now on my night table where I can smell them. Later he sent a gift of Belarusian weaving and a straw peasant doll.

Boris said if I were here longer I should get Zina to tell me the story of her life, which he said was very interesting. She was the oldest of Mendel's three children; there were a much younger sister and brother. The brother was killed in the war. The sister was deaf and didn't marry until very late in life, when someone asked for her hand when she was quite old. She did accept him, a "formal marriage," as Boris put it, and went to keep house for him.

According to Boris, Zina realized it was dangerous to stay in Zlobin when most of the other Jews refused to believe they were in any real danger from the Nazis. She managed to buy a couple of horses, and a cart into which she loaded her frail, aged father, who had diabetes, the two younger children, and herself. They made a long and dangerous journey to, I think it was, Kazakhstan, where they lived for four years under the most primitive conditions.

All the Jews who stayed behind were slaughtered, including the children. Jewish children were shot to death by Nazi soldiers.

It feels good just to lie in bed, dictate my journal, and not have to go anywhere. Yasha is very sweet and protects me. He's also, of course, extremely intelligent, and quickly figures out what I want and tries to please me. Boris, too, wants to please me, but he's oblivious to what I want; namely to be left alone because I feel sick.

I'm glad Yasha has some time to himself now. These days have been intense. And he's been speaking English and translating non-stop; that must be tiring.

Yasha says Boris seems to be fairly well off, compared to most people here, and I rather think so, too, after visiting his flat. It's modern and fairly comfortable, in local terms. He has no wife to support, though no doubt he helps his daughter. He has a stable position. Yasha didn't feel he was desperate for money, in fact he couldn't understand why he didn't do more for his mother, who seemed so poor. I thought she might refuse to accept much help. Of course we don't really know Boris's circumstances.

I'm happy to say Yasha found a gas station and was able to fill the tank of the Lada. This means we'll be able to drive around a bit tomorrow before heading for the airport, if I feel up to it.

Yasha says he feels ashamed of his country, for me, because there are so many problems. I said, "Yes, that's a bad feeling, to be ashamed of your country. But all countries have good things and bad things, including America."

En route to Gomel, I fed him bits of peanut butter on knekkebrod, which I'd brought from Sweden. To my surprise he said it was delicious. We shared a chocolate bar, which he also enjoyed, the first of the chocolate bars I've been carrying that I've so far tasted. I think I ate it because I wanted him to have some. And partly because my time in Streshin had been so profoundly intense, and I wanted something sweet.

When I awoke from my afternoon nap at six and came out into the living room, Cousin Boris was there, talking at a great rate with my landlady, Yeva. He presented me with yet another gift, a one-volume encyclopedia of Belarus with a lot of pictures of different rivers, and animals, and trees and so forth. The book is in Russian and weighs about ten pounds, but despite these drawbacks I believe it will be very useful if in fact I do write a novel set in Russia. I thanked him, and also for the flowers and other gifts.

We had a good discussion of the visa question. I told him that if he decides to emigrate after Sofa is settled in New York, I would be glad to help out by getting him a ticket. He thanked me, I gave him my card, and he filed it away for future reference. He said that, right now, his situation is actually good, as Yasha had guessed. He has a steady job. His son's work takes him abroad where he can acquire hard currency, and his daughter has a good friend in Belgium. So he feels his children will be all right. Of course he doesn't want to leave his mother, and she refuses to emigrate. She's too old and "conservative," as he put it. She has diabetes and various other ailments of old age. She doesn't want financial help. He said, "I help her with my hands," bringing her things and making repairs to her house. She's a rigid person, apparently, who always wants things in exactly the same place. I said this gives many old people a feeling of security, but Boris says she has always been this way. Boris has tried to persuade her to move to a better house, but she's absolutely unwilling.

None of this surprised me; it was what I had guessed.

Boris graciously said he would be very happy to meet my children, and extended an invitation to them to stay with him if they ever came to Belarus. I said I would pass this on to them.

Yasha returned from his outing to beautiful downtown Gomel, bringing me some medicine. I drank the foul-tasting concoction, making a face. I also had a cup of chicken noodle soup from a mix I brought with me. So far it has stayed down. Sometime this evening I felt the fever had left me, so I'm hoping to be more or less back to normal tomorrow.

I spent some time with Yasha looking through the encyclopedia Boris had brought me, getting an idea of the contents. A bird very like the heron is, informally, the national bird of Belarus. Many of the animals are similar to those in Vermont, like bears and porcupines (the wild animal most commonly encountered in the woods). Little Olga asked Yasha to get her a porcupine as a pet!

Yasha said there are many wolves, even now, and they do indeed attack human beings in the winter.

Parts of Belarus are marshland, like the Pripyat marshes in the south. These are quite extensive and were the hiding place of the partisans during the war. People walk through them carrying long poles with which they test the ground at every step. It is very danger-ous to walk through the marshes carelessly.

Right now I'm feeling that my stay in Russia is one day too long. I was ready to go home today. However, I couldn't have predicted this. I miss Joe. It'll be wonderful to see him; I wish he were here right now, so I could curl up and be held, without needing to talk. Soon. Two more nights.

The next morning, my last in Belarus, Yasha again had a stiff neck from sleeping in the Lada. I offered him a Tylenol, which he refused. "And you? How are you this morning?"

"Much better."

"Good, good," he said. "I am very glad to hear it, really."

"Really, why?"

"But you are our guest."

I laughed. "And you have to return me to my husband in good condition?"

I wanted to return to Streshin, revisit the Goldins, ask Avram to drive around the town with us and tell me more about it, and take additional pictures, but Yasha shook his head. The drive was an hour and a half each way, and if anything happened to the car I would miss my plane. Reluctantly, I had to admit he was right.

I asked to take Yeva's picture. She immediately changed her clothes, painted on a happy face, penciled in thin dark eyebrows, and combed out her brassy hair, which she had wound on curlers the night before. The photograph shows her standing beside Ya-sha, whose arms are folded across his chest. She clings to his arm with childlike trust; his wrist is slightly flexed, so although his hand is very close to Yeva's, the two do not quite touch. She smiles; his lips under the dark moustache are serious, and there is a hint of challenge in his small, slightly slanted eyes. Behind the two of them, the crystal sparkles in Yeva's china cabinet, on top of which stand Cousin Boris's roses.

Yasha and I took a short drive west to Kalinkovici, where Yeva's ancestors, she told us, are buried. She wanted to come along, but Yasha dissuaded her when I told him I didn't feel much like talking.

He said, "Yeva is rather—" He waved his hands. "Excitable."

"I like her very much," I said. "But whatever comes into her head comes out of her mouth, perhaps because she is lonely."

"No, she was like that always."

In Kalinkovici we climbed a knoll from which we could look down on the sinuous coils of the Dnieper. The air was dense with smoke. Beyond the river, gray billows erupted under a blazing sun as flames raged through the peat moss. We stood a long time in silence, staring down at the fire. No one was making any effort to put it out. Finally Yasha said, "It is a symbol of our country." Then he shrugged. "But maybe not. You know, after the burning the grass grows better. So I have hope."

On the way to the Gomel airport, he told me that Yeva has a possibility of teaching German in the schools this fall. I was really happy to hear it.

He stayed with me, gently attentive, until the last possible moment. His presence made everything easy. He asked what had been the most memorable part of my trip. After a moment's thought I said, "The visit to the Goldins in Streshin."

"For me, the same. My grandfather, too, lived in such a house. I'm glad I was there."

"It was like being in a time machine."

"Yes, a time machine to take you a hundred years."

He accompanied me to the security check, where we said our goodbyes. I was sad as I told him, "Thank you for everything—I can never repay you."

He smiled. "It has been a great honor for me to be your Virgil."

I opened my arms. He gave me a respectful hug. I stepped through the gate and was gone.

In the departure lounge, I thought about Yasha. He was in shock when I told him I'd left enough money in his apartment to pay for a ticket to America. He began to protest. I said, "Your plane could crash. Who knows if I am doing you a favor? You said you were a fatalist. This is fate. Accept it."

The money I left him, not a huge sum to me—less than four nights in an Intourist hotel—is for him the equivalent of two years' salary.

Yeva strove to the end to make me eat. I accepted a boiled potato. For her lunch she had the leftover soup she and Yasha had made me from my dried soup mix the night before. Beaming she said, "If you have one of these little packages, you don't have to cook the second day."

Will I ever write the book about my grandfather? If I do, Yasha wants me to send him a copy. We were together for four days, and he never annoyed me, which is amazing. I couldn't have had a more patient, intelligent, sensitive guide.

The suitcases have been trundled out to the plane on an ancient truck. The windows of this lounge are filthy, the plastic chairs grimy; orangey foam rubber erupts from the slashed upholstery. Across from me, two young girls wait patiently on a sofa. One sprawls with her head in the lap of the other, who gently brushes the recumbent girl's hair.

We are aboard. A space was found for me, though I have no seat reservation. People bring aboard enormous quantities of luggage. A girl leads a spaniel on a leash down the aisle.

In the flurry of taking my seat, I drop my visa without realizing it. A man leans down to pick it up, and silently hands it to me with a sardonic look.

My book has been checked through inside my suitcase, so I have nothing to read. No matter, it's a short flight. Unless, that is, the plane lands somewhere other than Moscow. Yasha said this happened to him once.

Just about five. The motors are revving up—we are moving, right on time.

VIII. Back in Moscow

We landed in Moscow a few minutes early. Using pantomime, I asked the young girl who had been brushing out her friend's hair in the departure lounge the way to the baggage claim area. She looked alarmed, hearing me speak English, but then said, "Baggage?" (The Russian word is similar to ours) and pointed me in the right direction.

I waited in the crowd, and my suitcase soon appeared. As I reached for it the girl, who must have been watching me, lifted it off the belt and, smiling shyly, placed it on my cart. I was very surprised and pleased. She returned quickly to her friends—or sisters? I managed to find my last chocolate bar, and presented it to her.

A taxi driver who spoke no English except for the words, "Five dollars," took me to the hotel.

I passed through gleaming glass and steel revolving doors into an opulent lobby. Hyatt-like, an atrium soared upward, and a glass-fronted elevator decorated with twinkling lights sped noiselessly up and down. The air was fragrant. Two young women, a pianist and a flutist, were playing Bach's "Air on a G String," ignored by a sprinkling of dark-suited businessmen. I was stunned. Could this be Russia? A menu in a gilded frame informed me I had my choice of two restaurants. A French chef was mentioned. God, it sounded good!

I dragged my luggage cart up to the counter, where an impeccably groomed young woman who spoke perfect English and looked like Miss Universe smilingly informed me that this was not my hotel. This was the Sheremetyevo Novotel. My hotel was the Sheremetyevo, period, on the other side of the highway. If I walked out the door I would see it.

Reeling from the effects of culture shock, yet unwilling to leave, I temporized by detouring through the Novotel gift shop. The headline on the *International Herald Tribune* trumpeted, "Dollar Skids to Record Lows, Pushing Stock Market Down."

I was back to the real world—or was I? Which was the real world anyway?

Trudging across the highway with my suitcases, I confronted a tall, grim, cement fortress. It frowned down at me without benefit of identifying sign. I was back in the Russia I'd come to know: dreary, ill-lit, a few faded signs stuck to the walls with shreds of yellowing scotch tape. After the shock of the Novotel, it was almost reassuring to find no one behind the service counter. Sighting down the length of it I descried, through a half-open door, three women smoking cigarettes.

Eventually I attracted their attention and managed, with marginal assistance, to check in. I received a chit I was to take up to the sixth floor and "give to woman."

In time the woman appeared, I gave it to her, and she led me down the hall and showed me into a bare room lit by a 25-watt bulb and containing two lumpy, narrow beds. On the nearer bed a jacket was draped, beside a bulging plastic bag.

I pointed. "What is this?"

"Woman," she shrugged, and gestured me toward the other bed.

Evidently I was to share the room with a stranger.

I turned into an American tourist instantly. "Oh no, there must be some mistake. I reserved a single room. I paid for a single room."

I knew it was useless, for she really couldn't speak English; but after glimpsing the Novotel across the road, the prospect of spending the night in this room suddenly seemed unendurable. I longed for a hot bath, for dinner in a decent restaurant, for the Air on a G String.

After some futile negotiation with the woman back at the service counter, in which she explained that I'd only paid forty-five dollars for my room, which I hadn't realized, and that this only entitled me to a bed, not a room to myself, I retraced my steps to the Novotel.

I felt guilty as I stood at the reception desk studying the list of charges—$149 for a room, $34 for the dinner I fancied, plus the cost of the telephone calls I intended to make. Such extravagance seemed immoral, even obscene, while the Russians who had befriended me were struggling with "the situation"; I could hear Boris Ioffe admonishing me, "Remember, two hundred dollars is a fortune to him. . ."

Miss Universe was waiting for me to make up my mind. "I'll take it," I said.

I shared the Novotel limo with a fat, dark-haired American couple with a slim, blond child of a year or so. I asked if they were going home after visiting the Soviet Union.

The young woman smiled. "Actually, we came to adopt this baby."

The father was holding the child, pulling down the little shirt that kept riding up over his tummy.

I said, "There must have been an incredible amount of paperwork."

She rolled her eyes. "My husband has been in Moldavia since July, and I've been here almost a month. Have you been visiting Moscow?"

"No, I just came back from Belarus."

"Oh, were you visiting friends?"

"Well, they're friends now."

"We feel that way, too. We made a lot of new friends."

As I was going through the final checkpoint in the Moscow airport, on the way to catch the plane to Stockholm, a security man examined my passport and visa and announced, "Visa finish."

"What?" I said, standing on tiptoe and applying my ear to the hole in the glass front of the booth. "I didn't hear you."

"Visa finish."

"I don't understand."

He raised his voice. "Visa finish August 25! Today is 26! Visa no good!"

Oh my god, I thought, is that possible?

He beckoned another militiaman over.

Then it hit me. Originally I'd been scheduled to fly from Gomel to Stockholm, on the 25th, but the second leg of the trip had been changed to the following day because there wasn't enough time to make my connection. Evidently the expiration date on the visa hadn't been corrected.

I felt really frightened. In twenty minutes my plane would be leaving. I started to explain, but the second officer, after taking a quick look at me, simply waved me through, to my relief. I hurried off to the departure gate, thankful I wasn't going to have to deal with god knows what.

After the Trip. Two weeks later, in Vermont. I drove through a big storm last night to have dinner with Bob and Mary Belenky at The Clearing and swap stories about Russia with Bob, whose stay overlapped mine though we didn't see each other. He spent the whole time in the bosom of a numerous family of cousins (it got to be a bit much, though most of the time he loved it, and them), and went with them to Smolensk, where his father came from. He arranged his trip via Intourist, with all the accommodations pre-planned, and had an official translator/guide. I felt rather superior about having gone on my own; I could see they were impressed. They decided Bob had had a wonderful visit, but I'd had an adventure.

True in a way, but also a bit of a fraud, because the people in the physics network took such wonderful care of me. But—I did go on the Moscow subway alone, twice, which Bob wasn't permitted to do; not to mention flying from Moscow to Minsk alone. That did feel adventurous, i.e. scary. I mean, for god's sake, what would have had to have happened for me to just say flat out, "It was an adventure"? A close brush with death? It was an adventure.

IX. Afterword

Friday, Sept. 11, 1992, Cabot. Two weeks now since I left Russia, and thoughts of the trip still obsess me. I wake up thinking about it. About the people. Fantasies of Yasha, Marina, and perhaps Olga coming to the U.S. and staying in our house while Yasha works at the University of Maryland. I came to love these people. But I have to remember that I can't control their lives, and it would be wrong to try. What I can do is let them know that if they ever want or need to leave Belarus, I will help them any way I can. Decisions are up to them. I don't know whether it would be wrong to try to influence them, even; to point out the instability of the situation there, the anti-Semitism that can always flare up and menace them—but don't they know these things better than I do? Of course. Who am I to butt in? And in the long run, who knows what is "good"? Who can foretell the future?

Yesterday I called Yasha in Minsk. It was seven in the morning there, and as usual I woke him up. But it's the only time you can get through. He sounded happy to hear from me, and told me it was his birthday. He didn't say my call was a gift, but I got the message. Only later did it hit me that his birthday is the same as Joe's—another coincidence. Marina had gotten her Ph.D. the day before, and was in Ukraine; I asked him to convey my congratulations. He hopes to go to Argonne "now that you have made it possible" in four months or so, and will write us a letter when his plans are definite. He told me again how much he'd enjoyed my visit.

I wonder which will really prove to be the family I found—"mine," or Yasha, Marina, and Olga.

The Dancing Woman
(Excerpt from pp. 92-94)

We stopped near the church and walked up a dirt road and I took a picture of it. It is unexpectedly grand for a small country town. I hadn't expected it to be so beautiful. If I ever go back to Streshin I'd like to walk around the church and go inside. Most incongruously, loud western dance music was pulsating through the air. I couldn't imagine why, but as I neared the church I saw, off to one side, a young blond woman dancing in a courtyard with a tiny child. I stood there in amazement, watching her. She danced on and on, rocking and rolling and shaking her hips, as the child stumblingly tried to imitate her, waving its tiny arms and looking about to tumble into the dust. I thought, "So there is life in Streshin."

I snapped a picture of the two of them, and then another. I am aware of Yasha, stiff as a sentry, watching me watch them. The woman seems lost in her dance, but suddenly as she whirls she catches sight of us, stops, and after a moment comes out to where we stand. She looks about thirty, with frizzed, bleached-blond hair, heavy blue eye shadow, a short, tight, denim skirt, and a see-through blouse trimmed with lace. She seems totally unlike anyone I've seen in Streshin.

Yasha tells her I've come from America, and she looks at him skeptically. "From America? You're kidding. Is she really?" Up close there is something world-weary about her; she is older than I thought. The loud music is still throbbing through the air. I feel a desire to make contact with her, directly. I wish I could talk to her, but that's impossible, so I reach out my hand. She takes it immediately. We look into each other's eyes. After a moment we find ourselves swaying to the music. Both of us laughing, we begin to dance, she in her tight denim skirt and sexy blouse, I in my travel-creased shirt and baggy pants, with my camera dangling from one hand and my WETA tote bag in the other. As the American music pounds and swells in the long shadow of the church, our dance grows faster and faster, a dance of reaching across miles, across years, across differences that are unfathomable; a dance of survival and joy, as when Miriam and her women danced with their timbrels along the shore of the Red Sea.

CPSIA information can be obtained at www.ICGtesting.com
Printed in the USA
BVOW10s0318041215

428990BV00001B/1/P